the new tea book

the new tea book

a guide to black, green, herbal, and chai tea

by sara perry
photographs by alison miksch

completely revised and updated
including over 50 delicious recipes

CHRONICLE BOOKS
SAN FRANCISCO

Library of Congress Cataloging-in-Publication Data:

Perry, Sara.
the tea book : a guide to black, green, herbal, and chai tea
/ by Sara Perry ; photographs by Alison Miksch.
p. cm.
includes index.
ISBN 0-8118-3053-5 (pbk.)
1. Tea. 2. Cookery (Tea) I. Title.
TX817.T3 P475 2001
641.6'372—dc21   00-052334

designed by **vivien sung**
prop styling by **barbara fritz**
food styling by **bettina fischer**

Printed in China

Distributed in Canada by Raincoast Books
9050 Shaughnessy Street
Vancouver, BC V6P 6E5

10 9 8 7 6 5 4 3 2

Chronicle books LLC
85 Second Street
San Francisco, California 94105

www.chroniclebooks.com

DEDICATION

To Arlene Schnitzer, my dear friend and favorite tea companion.

ACKNOWLEDGMENTS

Thanks go to the friends who generously shared their ideas, time, and recipes, especially Jane Zwinger, Kathlyn and Matthew Meskel, Bette Sinclair, Karen Brooks, and Larry Kirkland. To Jerry Balwin for his helpful advice and to Peet's Coffee & Tea, who provided a delicious array of teas for recipe testing. To Catherine Glass, whose confidence and advice are always invaluable, and to Amy Treadwell at Chronicle Books, who was always there, ready to help, with good advice and lots of cheer.

Finally, as always, my thanks go to Bill LeBlond, senior editor at Chronicle Books, for his trust, patience, and friendship.

contents

. . .

introduction

Tea is hot and getting hotter. From iced to spiced, from austere black tea to sweetened and milky chai, from a flowery pick-me-up to a healing herbal, no other beverage has such a place in the heart of every civilization. No wonder it is the most popular beverage in the world, next to water. Riding a new wave of popularity in the West, tea appeals to us in many ways. It offers Zenlike stimulation, serves as a consoling brew when we need a private moment, regularly elicits inspiration during creative sessions at the office, acts as a meeting ground between old friends, and boosts athletic performance. In *The New Tea Book,* you will discover the wide variety of teas that are available and their benefits, as well as the many beverages, savories, and delectable sweets that accompany tea or are made with it.

Like fine wines or single-malt Scotches, tea offers the discriminating palate subtleties of flavor and aroma and nuances of body and character, plus all the pleasures of exploring culture and provenance. *The New Tea Book* guides you as you discover the essential qualities of black, green, oolong, and herbal teas, from the full-bodied and faithful Assam to the bright and spicy Yunnan, from the fresh and grassy Sencha and sassy mints to the bittersweet and slightly smoky Gunpowder. You'll understand the benefits of drinking black and green teas, and you'll discover the curative and preventive powers of herbal teas, including the ways in which they fight off aging and enhance beauty.

When I was a child in California, tea was a magical drink I shared with my godmother. At her kitchen table, just big enough for the two of us, we'd sit and share a pot of English Breakfast tea, which she drank plain, and I drank sweetened with warm milk and honey. After Gracie poured my cup, I counted the bubbles that appeared on the surface. Miraculously, I found dimes equal to the number of bubbles when I lifted the saucer and looked underneath. Now I am hiding coins for a little boy named Dylan Paul, and although tea carries many associations for me, it will always remain a most magical beverage.

the history
and
cultivation of tea
. . .

The discovery of tea is lost among the folktales. Chinese storytellers recite the legend of Emperor Shen Nung, the father of agriculture and herbal medicine, who lived almost three thousand years before Christ and taught his people the value of cultivating land and the wisdom of boiling water to make it safe for drinking. One day, while working in his own garden, Shen Nung noticed the leaf of a camellia-like bush floating in his steaming bowl of water. Sipping the concoction, he discovered a drink that was refreshing and exhilarating.

For the Japanese, tea had its origin in an act of atonement rather than discovery. Their central character is the missionary monk, Daruma (Prince Bodhidharma), who brought Buddhism from India to China and Japan. In A.D. 520, Daruma began a nine-year meditation in a cave-temple near Canton, but, growing weary after many months of staring at a stone wall, he fell asleep. Awakening, Daruma was so displeased with himself that he cut off his lazy eyelids and threw them to the ground. It was there, according to legend, that the first tea plant grew, providing Daruma with an elixir that kept him alert during the remaining years of his reverie. The legend neatly echoes an almost identical and earlier Indian legend.

By the eighth century, tea was being eulogized in literature and legislation. The Chinese poet and scholar (and one-time acrobat) Lu Yu wrote the definitive commentary on tea. *Ch'a Ching,* known as *The Classic of Tea,* is still read today.

With each succeeding dynasty, tea evolved to reflect society. During Lu Yu's era, the T'ang dynasty (A.D. 618–906), tea enjoyed its golden age. The world's largest empire was a mecca for traders, and tea was a flavorful commodity. During this period, tea often was brought to Japan by monks returning from pilgrimages to China. Pounded and shaped into molds, tea bricks were easy to transport, and the beverage was made simply by breaking off a chunk into boiling water.

During the Sung dynasty (A.D. 960–1280), the refinements of tea culture blossomed in both China and Japan. Powdered tea and delicate porcelain came into vogue, and the first teahouses appeared. Many of the rituals used in the Japanese tea ceremony, *Chanoyu,* date to this elegant period.

Prized as a tonic and panacea, tea's shiny leaves were considered food by early Asian nomads. Some of the world's first energy bars were concocted by mixing tea leaves with salt, garlic, and dried fish. The reeking but portable result made a handy form of exchange. After the social, political, and cultural upheaval of Kublai Khan and his Mongol relatives, the Ming dynasty (A.D. 1368–1644) attempted to revive many lost rituals. The black, green, and oolong teas we are familiar with today were developed during this dynasty, and the teapot became an indispensable vessel for brewing.

As sixteenth-century Portuguese, Dutch, and other European traders and missionaries began to visit Asia, word of the beverage spread. The Dutch introduced tea to England in the early 1600s, but it remained the drink of aristocrats until the 1650s, when coffeehouses began serving tea as an alternative to coffee and hot chocolate. In 1657, Garway's Coffee House in London advertised tea as a cure-all, and rumors attributing Chinese longevity to tea drinking helped spread the gospel. But tea was considered a man's drink until King Charles II's consort, Catherine of Braganza, introduced tea at court as the fashionable breakfast drink.

Tea came to North America in the mid-seventeenth century, when the Dutch settled on the small island now known as Manhattan. The neighboring British colonies took longer to embrace the drink. In fact, they didn't drink it at all. Instead, they boiled the leaves and ate the lifeless vegetation with a little salt and butter.

Barely a hundred years after its introduction to Great Britain, tea had become an international commodity, but its popularity in America imploded due to an ill-conceived political maneuver. The British government levied a special tax on teas destined for the colonies, and the colonies protested with a boycott. As tea sales plummeted, the British tried to force the colonies to take the surplus, and, in a manner of speaking, they did. In December 1773, participants in the Boston Tea Party, one of many held in different ports, dumped the tea in the harbor and set the stage for the American Revolution. It was decades before Americans began to drink tea again.

The twentieth century proved to be a busy one for American tea enthusiasts and entrepreneurs. In the scorching summer of 1904, the United States was strutting her economic stuff at America's first World's Fair, held in Saint Louis. From around the world, countries came to exhibit their wares, and an Englishman by the name of Richard Blechynden set up a booth to promote Indian black tea. But no one was willing to drink his steaming brew in the sweltering heat. Out of desperation the frantic man poured the hot tea over ice and, to everyone's delight, a quenching new beverage—iced tea—was invented.

Four years later, Thomas Sullivan, a New York tea importer, initiated a second major innovation. Deciding to cut his overhead, he replaced the large sample tins of tea he sent to his retail customers with small, individual silk bags. Eventually, filter paper replaced the silk, and it's safe to say that tea bags are here to stay.

With the dawn of the new millennium, tea is more popular than ever. During the 1990s, tea sales more than doubled, reaching $4 billion a year in the United States, and iced tea continues to be second only to cola in popularity. One of the world's most popular beverages, tea has shown a sophisticated ability to transform itself. Long praised for its beneficial health components, tea is showing up in everything from cosmetics to candles, ointments, and balms.

growing tea

An old-fashioned bouquet of camellias and your grandmother's tea service have more in common than the sideboard on which they're standing. The tea bush and the camellia bush are kissing cousins, related by the scientific classification of genus. The familiar camellia plant, with its shiny, green leaves and lovely, corsage-like blossoms, is known as *Camellia japonica,* while the evergreen tea plant that supplies the world with its second most popular beverage is *Camellia sinensis.*

Native to Asia, the tea bush or shrub thrives in semitropical and tropical climates. Although its glossy, elliptical leaves grow quickly in a humid, junglelike environment, the best tea grows above five thousand feet, where harsher conditions encourage the leaves to mature slowly and develop complexity. Most cultivated tea is grown on large estates, plantations, or "gardens," but there are still postage stamp–sized plots, especially in China and Japan, where individual families grow enough for themselves, their village, and, when the price is right, export.

If left to grow wild, the tea plant can reach thirty feet in height or higher. (In the Yunnan province of China, there is an ancient tea "tree" that, at a hundred feet, towers over the landscape.) For commercial use, cultivated plants are pruned to waist height. Pruning encourages the dense growth of young shoots, called "flush," and makes the work of harvesting the crop easier.

Even though a great deal of tea production has been mechanized, the young shoots destined for finer teas are still handpicked. An experienced tea leaf plucker—usually a woman—can pick enough shoots in one day to produce nine pounds of finished tea, equal to eighteen hundred cups of tea, or the annual consumption of a thirsty Brit.

The number of leaves plucked from each shoot is one of the major factors that determine quality. The finest teas use only the flavorful top leaf and bud, while a coarse plucking grabs the first three, four, or five leaves on a sprig and produces a stronger, harsher brew. Mechanical harvesters pluck not only the top two leaves and bud but other leaves as well. The tea is then processed through a "cut, roll, curl" machine that results in broken leaf sizes.

With the variety of teas on the market, you might assume that there are many different kinds of tea plants. Until the nineteenth century, it was believed that green tea was made from one species and black tea from another, but thanks to noted botanist Sir George Watt, the different tea plants were identified as belonging to the same species. The dramatic differences among types of tea depend instead on where they're grown and harvested. The other crucial variable is how the tea is processed. The next chapter explains what's different about each variety, explores whether tea gives you a lift, and discusses the health benefits of tea (does green tea really prevent tooth decay?), along with many other facts vital to your selection of tea.

choosing tea

· · ·

When you buy tea from a supermarket, gourmet shop, Web site, or mail-order catalog, you're confronted with dozens of choices. How do you determine which tea you'll try next? Do you end up with the kind your mom used to fix whenever you were sick, or do you settle for the brand that's at eye level on your grocery store shelf? Or are you game to explore the tea of connoisseurs and savor the legendary teas from single plantations? One thing is certain: understanding how tea is grown and processed, recognizing the different categories, and knowing what goes into the various blends will make choosing your tea far more enjoyable and interesting.

If you were to try to brew a pot of tea with freshly picked tea leaves, you would face a somewhat bitter and watery drink. Just as a tea's quality depends on which teas are picked, its special character results from how the fresh tea leaves are treated after they've been harvested.

There are three major methods of processing freshly picked leaves, and each results in a different category of tea: green, black, or oolong. What sets these teas apart from one another is the amount of fermentation that is allowed to take place. Fermentation is a chemical reaction, specifically oxidation, that occurs between the air and the leaf's natural juices. However, unlike fermenting grapes, fermenting tea has nothing to do with microbes or alcohol.

green tea

Green tea's delicate, unfermented liquor most closely resembles the taste of the tea leaf in its natural state. Indeed, green teas like Gunpowder and Pearl Dew are often described as having a light, slightly sweet, herbaceous flavor, while others surprise the tongue with a smoky, maltlike flavor that leaves your mouth dry. Until the Ming dynasty (A.D. 1368–1644), green tea was the only type of tea produced in China, and it is still their most popular tea, although it makes up only 20 percent of the world's tea production.

The first step in processing green tea is to steam or pan-fire the freshly picked leaves. This destroys the natural enzymes necessary for fermentation. The steaming not only helps to preserve the leaves' natural oils and important natural antioxidants (also referred to as polyphenols and tannins), it also helps to soften the leaves, making them more pliable. After steaming, the leaves are rolled or twisted, which forces the cellular structures to break down so that they will release their aromatic juices when brewing occurs. A second gentle heating, also called firing, reduces the water content further, to 3 percent moisture. The rolling and firing may be done in two steps or repeated several times. The end result is that the leaves dry slowly.

The last step in processing green tea is grading—sorting the leaves according to shape and age. The choicest grade is Gunpowder. Its young leaves are rolled into tiny balls that resemble BB shot. Other grades include Young Hyson (middle-aged leaves that can be rolled or twisted), Imperial (older leaves made in the Gunpowder fashion), and several lesser grades, ending in dust.

Green teas are produced mainly in China, Taiwan, Japan, and India. Although many of the steps are mechanized, you can still find handmade teas in specialty stores, Asian markets, and on the Internet. Rolling tea leaves by hand is a tedious process. A worker goes over each of the leaf-laden trays two hundred times or more, rolling the leaves against the tray with his or her palms. How the worker rolls the leaves will determine whether the tea is twisted, curled, flat, or pellet shaped.

black tea

Black tea is familiar to anyone who has ever dunked a Lipton tea bag, enjoyed a spot of English Breakfast, or sipped a tall, frosted glass of iced Ceylon on a summer afternoon. Black tea's popularity surpasses all other teas in the Western world today.

The most processed of the three categories, black tea tastes the least like the natural leaf. Instead of being steamed, the harvested tea leaves are placed on large drying trays and allowed to wither until they are limp. Depending on the type of tea being produced, withering takes place either in the sun or in the shade. The leaves are then bruised and rolled either by hand or by machine, giving the air and the aromatic juices a chance to mix. Since the enzymes and bacteria are still present—they haven't been deactivated by steaming, as they are in green tea—fermentation begins in the humid, climate-controlled fermenting rooms. This fermentation/oxidation process takes just a few hours. Once the green leaves turn a coppery red—a color that tea specialists say reminds them of an apple turning brown after it's sliced—the leaves are ready to be dried (fired) to stop any further fermentation.

Unlike green tea, black tea is graded according to size, not quality. After the tea has received its final firing, it consists of a jumbled pile of whole leaves, broken leaves, bits of branches, and very small particles of tea dust. Mechanical or manual sifters with graduated mesh separate these pieces according to size, which not only gives the tea a better appearance but also ensures an even brewing time.

The two main grades of black tea are *leaf* and *broken*. Subdivisions of the leaf grade include Orange Pekoe (pronounced "peck-oh"), Pekoe, and Souchong. Each name refers to a particular size, color, or texture of the finished leaf. In the case of Orange Pekoe, the name refers to the larger leaves on a fine plucking, and not to an exotic flavor. The broken grade is divided into still smaller sizes, which are ideal for quick brewing and tea bags.

oolong tea

Oolong teas are treated in much the same way as black teas, but withering and fermentation times are minimized. While black teas are fully fermented, oolongs are only 75 percent fermented. This results in a deliciously fruity tea that evokes the qualities of both black and green teas.

Unlike black teas, oolongs are graded only according to their quality. The best is called Choice, followed by Finest to Choice, Finest, Fine to Finest, and so on, a bewildering array of superlatives that ends in Standard. Since there can be many crops in one year, the quality of an oolong refers not only to the character of the leaf and how it was handled but also to the time of year it was harvested and the part of the plant that was plucked. For example, the best Formosa Oolongs are harvested in the summer months. They usually carry the Finest grade, while the grades of the winter harvest, when the weather can be quite unstable, are usually Good to Standard.

Oolong tea originated in the Fukien province of China, where it is still manufactured today. Among tea specialists, Formosa Oolong, which is grown in Taiwan, is considered the best. Oolong tea accounts for less than 2 percent of the world's yearly consumption of tea.

You also may encounter two other categories of tea: pouchong tea, which is lightly oxidized and is classified between a green and an oolong tea, and white tea, a rare and expensive unoxidized tea that is similar to green tea.

blended tea

After tea is produced and graded, it is packed into aluminum-lined plywood chests and sold by tea brokers to companies that blend, package, and sell it. Whether loose or in tea bags, most packaged teas are a blend of many different teas. It is the tea blender's responsibility to maintain quality and consistency by blending teas to create the tastes you've come to expect or are about to discover.

scented tea and flavored tea

Scented and flavored teas have been around since the first tea drinkers decided their tea needed a little pizzazz. By adding the sweet or pungent flavor of fruit or spice, the fragrant scent of blossoming flowers, or, in the case of Lapsang Souchong, pine smoke, tea manufacturers are able to alter or enhance their tea.

Jasmine, chrysanthemum, gardenia, and magnolia are the most popular flowers used in scented tea. For centuries, making Jasmine tea has meant gathering fresh jasmine blossoms in the early morning, before they've bloomed. When evening comes and the blossoms open their heavily scented petals, they are either placed beside or mixed in with green or oolong tea leaves. After several hours, the dry leaves absorb the sweet aroma, and the entire process is repeated until the desired amount of aroma and flavor is absorbed. This method is still practiced, but technological innovations such as hot air blowers and combining machines help the blossoms spread their fragrance. You will sometimes find the spent blossoms in your tea.

Flavored teas, such as Orange, Peach, Vanilla, and Black Currant, are fast-rising stars on grocery store shelves. The scent or flavoring in these specialty teas is sprayed onto the leaves, which are gently heated to absorb the flavoring. Earl Grey is one of the nobler examples. Spiced teas, such as Orange Cinnamon and Lemon Spice, have spices and fruit rinds intermixed with the leaves to create their characteristic flavors.

Another popular tea product that's lining supermarket shelves and refrigerator cases is ready-to-drink canned and bottled teas, which are, more often than not, lemon-, strawberry-, peach-, or mango-flavored iced teas. Created to go head-to-head with soft drinks, they are marketed as more healthful than soft drinks and more thirst quenching. One look at the ingredients list and you'll discover that the sugar content is too close to that of soft drinks to be comfortable. And when it comes to taste, it's hard to find the tea flavor. There are exceptions, however; you just have to explore, sip, and savor.

popular teas and tea blends

With more than three thousand varieties of tea and countless combinations, your choice is staggering. Until recently, buying rare or single-garden teas was difficult, because most never reached your local marketplace. Times have changed, however, and so have the number of ways you and the tea merchant can search out and purchase fine tea. Even if you aren't dialed into e-commerce, the global community, or the Internet, they are bringing the world of tea to your doorstep.

Here is an introductory guide to some of the world's finest and most popular teas and tea blends. If you experiment, you'll discover that the way in which a tea has been grown and handled, as well as its grade, all contribute to its taste. Describing that taste can be elusive and, like fine wines and coffees, each tea has its signature characteristics.

green tea varieties

DRAGON WELL, also known as Lung Ching or Long Jing, is one of China's most noted teas. The leaves are long, flat, and a vibrant jade green. Dragon Well teas produce a clear, pale emerald-green tea with a slightly sweet, buttery, and lingering mellowness that will last through several infusions. It's ideal for those quiet, contemplative times.

GEN MAI CHA (gen-my-CHA) is a name you'll recognize from Japanese restaurant menus. It is a hearty, everyday green tea that is blended with toasted rice kernels to give it a nutty flavor, which goes especially well with Japanese cuisine.

GUNPOWDER refers to a Chinese grade of green tea that is rolled into small pellets. The Chinese refer to it as Pearl tea. Pinhead Gunpowder is made from choice young tips and buds. Because the leaves are tightly rolled, they stay fresh longer than other green teas. Tea drinkers enjoy the pale green brew, with its slightly grassy flavor. Be sure to brew it loose in your cup, so you can watch the leaves unfurl gracefully in the water. Gunpowder teas make a delicious afternoon tea and go well with any meal.

GYOKURO (ghee-OH-koo-roe) is a highly prized Japanese tea also known as Pearl Dew. It is grown in shaded gardens under marsh-reed screens, and only the tender top buds of the first flush are picked. These delicate leaves are high in chlorophyll and are made into a hand-rolled leaf that resembles pine needles. The tea has a deep green color and a rich, sweet, herbal flavor.

HYSON (HI-sun), also called Young Hyson, is named after an East India merchant who first sold it to the British. Originally made in China, Hyson is now made in India as well. Its tightly twisted yellow-green leaves produce a fuller-bodied liquor than most green teas.

MATCHA (MA-cha) is the ceremonial tea of Japan. It is made from the same leaf as Gyokuro, but it's dried in its natural shape and ground into a brilliant chartreuse powder. It is whisked with boiling water into a frothy, slightly thick, sweet, pleasant beverage.

SENCHA is a designation given to many teas from Japan, and it accounts for more than 70 percent of the country's export. It is the classic Japanese tea. A bright green tea, its flavor is reminiscent of freshly cut grass, and its aroma has a hint of the sea.

black tea varieties

ASSAM is the foundation for many of the finest tea blends. Grown in northeastern India (the world's largest tea-producing area), Assam's deep color and rich flavor make it an ideal tea whenever you want a full-bodied brew. Like the little black dress or the navy blue blazer, this is a basic tea that you will always want to have on hand.

CEYLON, now known as Sri Lanka, began growing tea in earnest when a fungus blight in 1869 wiped out the country's profitable coffee plantations. It was here that Sir Thomas Lipton made his fortune. Sri Lanka's mountain-grown teas, called *self-drinkers* because they are unblended, are among the world's favorites. Delicately flavored and bright in color, they can be enjoyed any time of day and are especially nice in the morning with milk. These teas also work very well when iced because they don't become cloudy when chilled. (See The Perfect Iced Tea, page 66.)

DARJEELING is called the champagne of teas. The finest of India's unblended teas, Darjeeling is grown on the slopes of the Himalayas in plantations called gardens. There are fewer than one hundred of these small-scale, family-based gardens clustered in the seven valleys of the Darjeelings.

True Darjeelings are still processed the way they were a hundred years ago. Like other exquisite teas, more Darjeeling is sold each year than is grown. To be sure you're buying a true Darjeeling and not an impostor from the lowlands, buy from a tea specialist knowledgeable in single-garden or estate teas (see "Resources," page 117).

Darjeeling's bright, golden-red color is attractive in the cup. Its teas have a delicate, flowery aroma, with the character and body to make the tea enjoyable to drink any time of day.

KEEMUN is the famous China black tea that connoisseurs refer to as the burgundy of teas. The small, tightly curled black leaves unleash a lovely red color when brewed, and the tea has a full, strong body. Its aroma is variously described as

smoky or as having an orchid bouquet. Excellent with food, this is a delicious breakfast tea.

LAPSANG SOUCHONG is the popular, smoky south China tea, recognizable the moment the tin is opened or the first cup is poured. Its pungent flavor comes from smoking the leaves over pine wood. Lapsang Souchong was a favorite with Western pioneers and trappers, and it's very pleasing at the office, served black or with milk and sugar.

PU'ERH (POO-air) is a Chinese black tea that is allowed to decay partially during the withering stage, permitting bacteria to enter the leaf and alter the flavor. The leaves are then buried and aged in the ground. The taste is earthy and very strong. The tea can be sold loose or compressed into cakes.

YUNNAN (YOU-nahn) is a pleasantly assertive Chinese tea from the southwestern province of Yunnan, where tea has been produced since the second century A.D. The long green leaves with their golden tips (a sign of meticulous plucking) make a rich, slightly floral, spicy taste that complements highly seasoned foods and is delicious when iced.

oolong tea varieties

FORMOSA OOLONG's peachlike aroma and fruity flavor are a result of shortened withering followed by partial fermentation. It is a nice complement to sweets and is enjoyable as an afternoon tea with scones and tea cakes or after a meal with dessert. Originally grown on the island of Taiwan by Chinese who longed for their native oolongs, Formosa Oolong has surpassed the native oolong in taste and reputation. It is one of the few commercially grown teas still produced on family farms.

TI KUAN YIN is a Chinese oolong from the Fukien province. Its curled leaves create an amber liquid and a delicate, peachy, slightly nutty flavor.

favorite tea blends

ENGLISH BREAKFAST starts many a sleepyhead's day and is especially good with a dash of milk. Once made from a self-drinking (unblended) Keemun, its strong, full-bodied flavor now often comes from a blend of teas from India and Sri Lanka.

IRISH BREAKFAST is a heartier brew than its English cousin because of the higher percentage of Assam and Sri Lanka teas. Like English Breakfast, it handles the addition of milk and sugar with grace.

RUSSIAN-STYLE BLENDS have a common characteristic: a striking aroma that most often comes from the addition of Lapsang Souchong. These exotic blends also include Keemun and China or Formosa Oolongs.

favorite flavored and scented teas

EARL GREY's signature ingredient is bergamot, a fragrant essence made from the rind of a citrus fruit (*Citrus bergamia*). Not all Earl Grey teas incorporate the same blend of black teas or the same amount of essence. It's worth experimenting to find the subtle balance of flavor versus fragrance that you like best.

JASMINE tea is highly fragrant and deliciously floral. It is made by gently scenting green or pouchong tea leaves with fresh jasmine as they are drying.

the components of tea

No matter what kind of tea you drink—black, green, or oolong—each shares components that affect how you feel and what you taste and smell. The main components of tea are caffeine, polyphenols (tannins), and essential oils.

Tea's pleasant lift comes from caffeine, a mildly habit-forming drug appearing naturally in many plants (tea, coffee, and cocoa, to name a few). People who drink tea often boast to their coffee-loving rivals that their beverage has half the caffeine of that high-octane bean. Sorry folks, that's not the case, but you can still feel smug. Let me explain. By weight, in its dry form, a pound of black tea has twice the caffeine as the same amount of coffee. What's the catch? You make two hundred cups from a pound of tea and only forty cups per pound of coffee.

The amount of caffeine in tea depends on the plant and the way it is processed. Fermentation also increases the amount of caffeine that makes its way to your cup. Since green tea is not fermented, it has the least caffeine. Here's a quick comparison: A six-ounce cup of drip coffee contains 70 to 180 milligrams of caffeine; a six-ounce cup of black tea has 25 to 110 milligrams, while oolong contains 12 to 55 milligrams, and green tea has 8 to 16 milligrams. To learn more about caffeine in tea, how it affects your body and your health, and ways to cut down, check out the next section, "Tea and Health."

A tea's color, pungency, and body come from polyphenols, also referred to as tannins. These components are present in every leaf, but the tender new growth, consisting of two leaves and a bud, is almost three times richer in polyphenols than the older leaves.

During fermentation, some of the polyphenols are oxidized and become water soluble. These polyphenols give tea its distinctive color. The unoxidized polyphenols, those that are not fermented, give tea its pungency. Because green tea is not fermented and its polyphenols are unoxidized, it is pale and has less body than black or oolong, but it tends to be more pungent. On the other hand, fermented black tea gets its rich, amber color from the oxidized polyphenols and, because it has fewer unoxidized polyphenols, is less pungent than green tea. As with much of life, however, generalizations don't tell the entire story.

The essential or aromatic oils give tea its fragrance and flavor. The oils are also known to aid in digestion because they stimulate peristalsis. In green tea, the flavor comes from the unfermented oils. In black tea, it comes from oils changed during oxidation. Therefore, in oolong tea, the fragrance and flavor come from a combination of unfermented and fermented oils. When these essential oils come into contact with your brewing water, they evaporate, giving you their elusive gift. When you brew a cup of tea properly, the caffeine, polyphenols, and essential oils interact and combine to make a tantalizing drink that, next to water, is the most popular beverage on earth.

tea and health

Over the centuries, tea has been considered a healthy beverage as well as a pleasurable one. Its therapeutic powers have long been glorified by scholars, scientists, and journalists. Lu Yu, the Chinese tea scholar, described tea in A.D. 780 as a cure for headaches, aching limbs, constipation, and depression. Today, medical journals throughout the world report that tea, especially green tea, stimulates mental clarity, reduces the risk of certain cancers and heart disease, lowers blood sugar levels, and helps to prevent viral infections, bad breath, and tooth decay.

A primary reason for tea's preventive powers, which applies to all types of teas, is strictly hygienic. In many cases, today as in ancient times, tea is safer to drink than water because it's boiled first, killing any disease-carrying bacteria. This is certainly advantageous, but let's look at some other health concerns, bad and good, associated with tea.

Caffeine in tea is a health issue for many tea drinkers. Tea does contain caffeine in moderate quantities. A naturally occurring drug, caffeine gives you a pleasant lift and revives the spirits. It stimulates the central nervous system, its levels peaking within an hour of reaching the bloodstream. Because it also has a stimulating effect on the kidneys, caffeine is a mild diuretic. It is mildly stimulating to the respiratory system as well—one reason that many athletes hydrate their bodies by drinking tea before they exercise.

Research has yet to confirm any ominous diseases related to the moderate use of tea, although health providers advise women suffering from severe fibrocystic disease and people with high blood pressure not to ingest much caffeine. If you're concerned and would like to cut down on caffeine, you're one jump ahead by choosing tea as your beverage. As noted in the previous section, all teas, especially green teas, contain less caffeine per cup than coffee. If you want to lower the caffeine still further, there are two simple ways to cut down: buy decaffeinated tea, or make a "second potting."

A second potting is simply the second pot or cup made from the tea leaves. Once boiling water touches the tea leaf, the caffeine it contains begins to dissolve. After a three-minute infusion, half of the caffeine will have dissolved into the water. By removing the tea leaves (another reason a tea infuser is handy) and using them to make your second pot, you will have effectively cut down on the caffeine.

Recently, the Western world has taken a greater interest in the health benefits of green tea. Research scientists are confirming what the Chinese knew centuries ago: the naturally occurring compounds found in green teas (and herbal teas) help to promote good health. As I mentioned earlier, green teas are high in unoxidized, and therefore unaltered, polyphenols. These polyphenols have strong antioxidant properties. Antioxidants help control the activity of free radicals, unstable molecules that damage cell structures and are implicated in a host of illnesses, including cancer and cardiovascular disease.

One of the most powerful polyphenols, found only in green tea, is epigallocatechin gallate (EGCG). Studies indicate that EGCG's antioxidant effect can be more powerful than that of vitamin E. The polyphenol also has been shown to keep influenza viruses in check. Another plus is that EGCG inhibits the growth of the bacteria that cause halitosis. (That's one reason the Japanese traditionally drink green tea after a meal.)

Tea, especially green tea, is also a rich source of fluoride. In fact, green tea contains more fluoride than fluoridated water. Tea has minerals such as manganese, the vitamins C, B2, D, and K, and a number of amino acids. Clearly, tea is one of those earthly wonders that's delicious and good for you. If you're interested in learning more about the health benefits of tea, I've listed several books in the "Resources" section (page 117).

herbal teas

When is a tea not a tea? When it's an herbal infusion, or *tisane*. Technically speaking, only a beverage made from the leaves of one plant, *Camellia sinensis,* can truly be called tea. If that's the case, what is an herbal tea?

Broadly speaking, all teas are herbal, since an herb is any plant, shrub, or tree capable of affecting our lives through its aroma, taste, flavor, or therapeutic use. True teas, made from *Camellia sinensis,* use the leaves and buds to create their brew. Herbal teas encompass a variety of plant parts, from leaves and flowers to roots and bark. Processed in much the same way as green tea, these plant parts are dried soon after harvesting to avoid any fermentation.

When you make a pot of herbal tea, follow the same basic rules you use for making tea: use clean utensils; start with cold, good-tasting water and heat it to the correct temperature; use the correct amount of tea and the correct brewing method; make sure you brew for the proper length of time; and serve your tea fresh. These rules are discussed in detail in the next chapter.

When you brew herbal tea, keep in mind that different plant parts require different brewing times. (Remember, because black, green, and oolong teas all use only the leaves of one plant, the amount of tea required for each cup tends to be uniform. This is not true of herbal teas.)

As a rule, when you make an herbal tea with leaves, use 2 rounded teaspoons of fresh leaves or 2 teaspoons of dried leaves for 6 to 8 ounces of boiling water. Depending on your preference, steep the tea for 5 to 10 minutes. If you are using plant parts such as roots, stems, and bark, you'll be making a decoction. In a decoction, instead of steeping or infusing the leaves, you simmer the coarse plant parts for up to 30 minutes to extract their flavors and components. (When a decoction is made for medicinal purposes, the tea is concentrated by reducing the liquid up to 30 percent.)

Speaking of decoctions, have you ever wondered what the difference is between an herb and a spice? It's not always clear, especially when it comes to tea.

Herbs tend to be more delicate and subtle in flavor and usually come from the leafy parts of the plant, while spices, known for their exotic, intense flavors, come from the bark, roots, seeds, and fruits. When you make tea from a spice, decoction is the method most often used because the components are more difficult to release.

Today's market of commercially available herbal teas continues to grow as people seek alternative drinks. Like traditional tea, a particular herb can be a self-drinker, or it can be blended with other herbs to make a beverage that unites the flavors of them all. Tea companies are developing new herbal beverages by combining teas with natural juices or sparkling water to make drinks that go as well with meals as they do on the football field or golf course. (Herbal teas and juices are high in potassium, making them an ideal isotonic sports beverage.)

On the following pages, you'll find some of today's most popular herbs, with a brief description of their effects plus instructions on how to brew each one into a tea. (Caution: When brewing herbs that you've gathered, do not use roadside herbs, which may be coated with noxious car exhaust, or herbs that may have been sprayed with pesticide.) You'll also find recipes for herbal tea blends and beverages as well as herbal recipes to transform your home and bath. Soothing, stimulating aromatic herbs—they are all here.

BASIL (*Ocimum basilicum* varieties) may be one of the tastiest herbs in Italian cuisine, but its fragrant green leaves also make a soothing infusion to help calm an upset stomach and quell nausea. Its tea has a clovelike flavor with peppery, mint-like undertones. Use 1 tablespoon of the fresh leaves or 2 teaspoons dried in 6 to 8 ounces of boiling water. Steep for 10 minutes.

CATNIP (*Nepeta cataria*) is a mouser's delight, and its scalloped leaves produce a subtle, lemony, mintlike tea, which the British drank before China tea came to their isles. Belonging to the mint family, catnip, when infused into a tea, helps to settle upset stomachs and was a traditional cold and flu remedy. Use 1 tablespoon of the fresh leaves or 2 teaspoons dried in 6 to 8 ounces of boiling water. Steep for 10 minutes.

CHAMOMILE (*Chamaemelum nobile,* Roman or English chamomile; *Matricaria recutita,* German chamomile) makes a comforting herbal tea with a light, sweet, applelike taste. A popular herb, chamomile is used as a base for many commercially blended herbal tea mixes. An infusion of the daisylike flowers used for the tea relieves nausea and anxiety and, if taken before bedtime, promotes sleep. Use 1 tablespoon of the fresh flowers or 2 teaspoons dried in 6 to 8 ounces of boiling water. Steep for 3 to 4 minutes, or up to 30 minutes for its medicinal effects. If you are allergic to ragweed pollen, it's best to avoid chamomile, since they are related.

GINSENG (*Panax quinquefolius,* American ginseng; *P. ginseng,* Korean or Chinese ginseng) has been proclaimed an aphrodisiac and cure-all for many human ailments. Its root often resembles the human form, indicative, some believe, of its curative powers. To make a decoction, use 1/2 teaspoon of the powdered root in 6 to 8 ounces of boiling water, simmering for 10 minutes.

HOPS (*Humulus lupulus*) are small, conelike flowers that flavor and preserve beer. The mellow and peppery tea made from hops is believed to work as a mild sedative that relieves tension. Use 2 teaspoons of the fresh flowers or freezer-dried hops in 6 to 8 ounces of boiling water. Steep for 5 minutes or to taste.

LAVENDER (*Lavandula spica, L. vera, L. angustifolia, L. officinalis*) is one of the world's favorite herbs. Its aromatic flowers have scented baths and given fragrance to perfumes and potions since ancient Roman times. As an herbal tea, it has a slightly sweet, highly aromatic flavor. It's often used as an accent in blends. (Peet's Coffee & Tea makes a delightful Earl Grey with Lavender. See "Resources," page 117.) Lavender is said to relieve fatigue, depression, and tension headaches. Use 2 teaspoons of the fresh flowers or 1 teaspoon dried in 6 to 8 ounces of boiling water. Steep for 3 to 5 minutes.

LEMON BALM (*Melissa officinalis* varieties) grows like a weed in many gardens. Infused into a hot beverage, it is valued for its restorative effects. Its lemony and invigorating infusion helps ease the stuffiness of a cold or the flu, as well as soothing nerves and aiding in digestion. Use 1/4 cup of the fresh leaves or 2 teaspoons dried in 6 to 8 ounces of boiling water. Steep for 5 to 10 minutes or to taste.

MINT (*Mentha* species), the ice cream of herbal beverages, comes in a plethora of pleasing flavor variations. Ancient Greeks and Romans spiked their dinner- and bath-water with mint sprigs. In medieval times, the herb was tossed on floors and trampled to sweeten stale rooms. Mint flavors range from peppermint to spearmint to apple, pineapple, and orange mint. The tea is a frequent home remedy for upset stomachs, headaches, and tension. Use 1 tablespoon of the fresh leaves or 2 teaspoons dried in 6 to 8 ounces of boiling water. Steep for 5 to 10 minutes or to taste.

PARSLEY (*Petroselinum crispum*) may be your splash of color on an otherwise dull dinner plate, but the hot beverage made from its fresh leaves is a tasty way to keep your breath clean, your joints limber, and your kidneys working. Parsley tea tastes the way it smells and is a great source of vitamin C. Use 1 tablespoon of the fresh leaves or 2 teaspoons dried in 6 to 8 ounces of boiling water. Steep for 5 to 10 minutes or to taste.

ROSE (*Rosa* species) petals make a lovely, aromatic brew if they are fragrant. It's the red-orange fruit, or hips, that people seek when they have a cold. The fruit of the dog rose (*Rosa canina*) is especially high in vitamin C—a single cup more than equals an armload of oranges. Rose hip tea has a pleasant, mildly tart, and fruity taste. Use 1 tablespoon of the fresh petals or 2 teaspoons dried in 6 to 8 ounces of boiling water. Steep for 5 to 10 minutes or to taste. Grind rose hips in a clean coffee grinder and infuse, using 1 teaspoon to each cup of hot, not boiling, water, to retain the vitamin C. Steep for 5 to 10 minutes.

ROSEMARY (*Rosmarinus officinalis*) is a powerful herb that has been a symbol of fidelity, friendship, and remembrance since antiquity. The tea tastes the way the potent herb smells. It is an all-around digestive and is also comforting, especially when you feel a cold coming on. Rosemary is often combined with other herbs into tea blends. Use 1 tablespoon of the fresh leaves or 2 teaspoons dried in 6 to 8 ounces of boiling water. Steep to taste.

SAGE (*Salvia officinalis*) tea has been used as a digestive aid since Hippocrates' time. Today, people drink the highly aromatic tea to help alleviate the flulike symptoms of a bad cold. As the name implies, this tea supposedly keeps your brain sharp and your memory quick. Use 1 tablespoon of the fresh leaves or 2 teaspoons dried in 6 to 8 ounces of boiling water. Steep for 5 to 10 minutes or to taste, and serve with lemon.

THYME (*Thymus vulgaris; T. x citriodorus,* lemon thyme) is a culinary herb that enhances the flavor of many savory dishes and is essential to a bouquet garni. Thyme's leaves and flowers also make a pungent, slightly bitter tea that is best enjoyed with honey and is believed to help relieve headaches, sore throats, and irritable bowels. Use 1 tablespoon of the fresh leaves or up to 2 teaspoons dried in 6 to 8 ounces of boiling water. Steep for 5 to 10 minutes or to taste.

chai

In much of the world, the word *chai* simply means tea. In the Western world, especially in North America, chai (rhymes with "high") has come to mean a tea brewed with spices, steamed or warm milk, and something sweet, such as honey, sugar, or flavored syrup. In India, where the drink originates, it is known as masala chai, and wherever people congregate, you'll find turbaned tea vendors—*chai wallahs*—selling their own particular chai brew in disposable, unglazed, clay cups or, less romantically, Styrofoam cups.

On the menus of coffee stores, cafés, and carts, chai has joined the club of chic hot drinks and shares equal billing with lattes and other steamed-milk beverages. As a morning riser or afternoon pick-me-up, chai's peppery and refreshing taste is a great energizer. A palate cleanser, chai has none of coffee's aftertaste.

Masala is an Indian word that refers to a combination of popular Indian spices used in the subcontinent's cuisine. Most of the time, the spice mixture is made by the cooks themselves for their own use. Traditionally, at least four—and usually more—spices are combined from a constellation of choices that includes cinnamon, cardamom, ginger, cloves, pepper, allspice, fennel, and star anise.

In India, masala chai is made with black tea. The street tea sellers use low-grade black teas or tea dust because they're cheap to buy and the strong flavor holds up to the seasonings and milk. While black tea is the traditional tea used in chai, green teas and herbs are also becoming popular, especially in North America.

One of the reasons for the delightful taste of chai is the milk. Whole milk gives the richest, most balanced taste, but many chai lovers use condensed milk or unsweetened evaporated milk. Lactose-intolerant or vegan appetites like their chai with soy or rice milk. In India, they may use water buffalo milk. Any of these work well, but do stay away from insipid fat-free dairy products.

With great-tasting chai beverages readily available in coffee shops and supermarkets, as well as dry mixes and recipes (see page 64) you can stir up at home, there's no excuse to keep this marvelous drink too far from your lips.

preparing tea

. . .

There are a variety of ways to brew tea, from the Mongolian practice of pulverizing tea leaves and boiling them with salted milk to the aesthetic Japanese ceremony of whisking powdered tea into a sea-green foam. Western tea drinkers follow the Chinese method of combining tea leaves with boiling water. While the method is simple and straightforward, there are several essential steps you should follow. Easy as they seem, they are crucial to a good cup of tea. On the following pages, each step is described in detail, along with some interesting information to help you make your perfect cup of tea.

❖ MAKE SURE YOUR KETTLE AND TEAPOT ARE CLEAN

❖ USE GOOD-TASTING, COLD WATER

❖ USE THE CORRECT AMOUNT OF WATER AT THE RIGHT TEMPERATURE

❖ USE THE CORRECT AMOUNT OF THE BEST TEA YOU CAN BUY

❖ BREW THE TEA FOR THE PROPER LENGTH OF TIME

❖ SERVE IT FRESH

make sure your kettle and teapot are clean

The freshest water and the finest tea can quickly be ruined if your utensils aren't clean. Even though your kettle is used only for boiling water, it needs to be washed and dried occasionally, since constant use can build up mineral deposits, giving an off taste to any water you put into it.

Have you ever noticed a brownish haze on the inside of your favorite teapot or travel thermos? That residue adds a bitter taste to your brew. Washing your teapot in a mild detergent or baking soda, and using a soft brush, sponge, or cloth to wipe out the inside will take care of the problem. Make sure that you completely rinse out any detergent; otherwise, the delicate bouquet of your favorite Darjeeling will taste suspiciously like a pan full of sudsy dishes.

use good-tasting, cold water

If the water you use to brew your tea tastes good, you're halfway there. If you're using tap water, let the cold water run briefly before filling your kettle. Tap water loses oxygen when it's left standing in water pipes for several hours.

If you don't like the taste of your tap water, experiment with different bottled spring or filtered waters until you find one whose taste you enjoy. Brita makes a filtration pitcher as well as a device that you can add to your faucet that removes chemicals like chlorine, which give an off flavor to water. The pitcher is inexpensive and widely available. By the way, don't use distilled water, the kind you use in an iron. It lacks minerals and tastes like air.

After you have placed your kettle on the stove to boil the water, preheat your teapot with warm water. When your kettle water has almost reached a boil, pour out the warm water in your teapot and your cups, and add your tea.

use the correct amount of water at the right temperature

How much boiling water do you need to make a proper cup of tea? Many instructions simply state "Add a bag or a teaspoon of tea leaves per cup of boiling water." What is a cup? To many of us, it's the 8-ounce mug we use at the office. To the tea expert, it's 5½ or 6 ounces. For the purposes of this book, we'll stick to 6 ounces. To be sure your pot of tea is perfect, check to see how many 6-ounce cups it takes to fill it.

The correct water temperature for steeping most green tea leaves is between 160°F and 175°F, depending on the specific tea. Oolongs are steeped at between 180°F and 190°F. Black teas need a full, rolling boil (212°F). The first time you brew a new tea, use a simple candy thermometer to check the water temperature. After that, you'll be able to judge it visually or by its sound. At 160°F, the water is restless but not yet simmering. At 190°F, bubbles are rising across the entire surface and the water is starting to steam. A rolling boil is self-evident.

use the correct amount of the best tea you can buy

Use 1 teaspoon of loose tea for each cup. The first time you try a new tea, use a measuring spoon. After you've measured the tea leaves correctly, place the leaves in the spoon you're apt to use every day. That way you'll always be able to gauge the right amount of tea and prepare the proper strength. And don't worry about adding an extra spoonful "for the pot." It's not necessary, and the end result is simply a stronger brew.

Unless the teapot has a built-in tea strainer, I like to use a stainless steel, wire-mesh tea ball to hold loose tea. I fill it only half full so the leaves have enough room to expand. (I'll use two balls if I'm making a large amount.) The ball can be removed easily when brewing is finished. After you have measured the amount of tea you're going to use and placed it in your pot, add the boiling water.

THE ROMANCE OF THE LEAVES. Tea bags screen from sight one of the subtle pleasures of tea drinking. Enveloped in filter paper, the finely cut leaves just lie sedately under the covers. But when loose tea and boiling water meet, it's a full-blown romance. Tea leaves come in myriad shapes, sizes, and textures, and all it takes is a little persuasive hot water to unwind and unveil their secrets. It's a performance worth watching, and it's always different, depending on the tea you use.

THE CONVENIENCE OF THE TEA BAG. While most guidelines discuss brewing tea with loose leaves, the number of tea drinkers using tea bags continues to grow. More than 50 percent of the tea consumed in the United States is made from tea bags, while in the British Isles the amount hovers at 30 percent.

Whether you're at home or in a restaurant, tea bags offer no-muss, no-fuss convenience in today's world of fast-food eating. And many tea companies have responded to demands from knowledgeable tea consumers by using high-quality tea in their bags.

When you purchase tea bags, it's better to buy smaller amounts or individually packaged tea bags. (Not the best environmental advice, I admit.) The reason is that the finely cut tea leaves used in most commercial tea bags have a greater surface area and become stale sooner than whole leaves.

Whenever you purchase tea in bags, keep in mind that the best tea does not necessarily mean the most expensive. It's true that fine teas cost more, but it's also true that expensive does not necessarily mean top quality. Many tea drinkers pay a premium for those lovely, imported tins whose packaging proclaims their reputation, but well-educated American tea agents are buying directly from the same quality sources on the world market and selling their tea for less.

FOR THOSE WHO WANT THE BEST. Keep in mind that most teas, whether loose or in a tea bag, are not premium teas. Most are casually swallowed without a moment's concern. It's similar to drinking a cup of preground canned coffee versus enjoying a cup of freshly ground Italian roast. However, once you taste the difference, it's hard to return to the inferior stuff. If you take the time to experiment with different teas and learn about the teas you like, you can make an informed decision about the kind of tea you buy. If you don't have a local tea shop that carries premium teas, a number of excellent sources of tea and information are available on the Internet or by mail-order catalog. Check out the "Resources" section, page 117, for some listings.

brew tea for the proper length of time

Don't simply dunk a tea bag in boiling water until the water turns brown. Tea leaves need sufficient time to open. Depending on the leaf size, that can be between 1 and 3 minutes for green teas, and 3 to 5 minutes for blacks. Even though the color of a tea is the first sign of brewing, its darkness doesn't necessarily reflect its strength. While black teas such as a Ceylon or Assam brew to a rich brown, a perfectly brewed green Sencha tea will turn only a pale yellow-green.

The time it takes for tea to brew really depends on the leaf size. The smaller the leaf, the faster the tea infuses. The smaller-leafed Assam and English

Breakfast teas and the ubiquitous tea bag infuse within 3 minutes. The medium-sized Ceylon takes closer to 5 minutes. Green teas that are tightly rolled or twisted take longer than those that are open.

Using leaf size as a guide, you'll need to experiment with your own tea to find its ideal brewing time. Notice the aroma while the tea is brewing, but be sure to watch the clock. If you let your tea steep too long, bitter qualities will come through and the tea will taste stewed.

serve it fresh

When it comes time to serve, remove the tea leaves by lifting out the tea bag or ball. If you put loose tea in your teapot, simply place a strainer between the spout and your cup to catch the leaves when you are ready to pour. Then give your tea a quick stir to blend the flavors and ensure an even strength. Serve in cups rinsed with hot water, and savor.

To keep tea hot temporarily, cover your teapot with a padded tea cozy. At work, I use a thermos-style carafe. It works very well—and therefore, so do I. By the way, I never keep coffee in my tea carafe. (I have a separate one for Juan Valdez's favorite brew.) Reheated tea loses its pizzazz and its flavor suffers. Once hot tea has turned cold, it's best to enjoy it iced—or make ice cubes out of it to give iced tea more flavor without diluting its strength or to give a surprising tang to fresh juices.

One more bit of advice. Whether you like black, oolong, or green tea, whether you use one rounded teaspoon or two, whether your water is at a rolling boil or a soft simmer, making a great-tasting tea is not about following the exact rules; it's about what tastes good to you.

milk, lemon, sugar, or plain?

If well prepared, your tea needs nothing more than for you to enjoy it. Whether you add anything else is really a matter of taste and tradition. In China and Japan, people prefer their oolong and green teas plain, while the British serve their freshly brewed black teas with a pitcher of milk. In Russia, a dollop of raspberry jam makes the sweetest of teas, and a slice of lemon is often used to brighten Russian tea.

As a rule, you'll find that oolong and green teas are best served plain, while brewed black teas often are enhanced by additional flavorings. The most commonly used flavorings you're likely to come across are milk, lemon, and sugar.

Milk's popularity in tea dates back to a seventeenth-century British custom. Until that time, tea had been served in heavy pewter or earthenware cups. When porcelain cups came into British vogue, milk was added because it was feared that adding hot black tea directly to the delicate china cup would cause it to crack. This wasn't the case, but, like the porcelain cup, adding milk became a hard habit to break.

Milk reacts chemically with tea. One of its proteins, called casein, binds with certain polyphenols, giving your tea a smoother, less astringent taste. (Polyphenols—or tannins—determine the color, flavor, pungency, and medicinal value of tea; see page 30.) With the full-bodied black teas grown in India and Sri Lanka, milk has a mellowing effect and, some say, actually enhances the flavor.

You'd think adding milk to tea would be a simple task, but entire essays and chapters have been devoted to the how and when of it. It all boils down to two choices: If you pour the milk first and then add the tea, they will blend without so much as a stir. If you add the milk afterward, you'll have more control over the amount of milk you use. Also, and this is getting picky, your cup stays warmer—and so does your tea—if you pour in the hot tea first, followed by the milk.

You'll find that it takes only a teaspoon or two of milk to flavor your tea. If you add more milk, the casein binds with all of the tannins and oppresses the character of the tea. If you run out of milk, don't try cream. It may come from the same

cow, but it's no substitute. True cream doesn't have as much casein, so its effect is quite different. It doesn't bind and so does not really complement your tea.

Lemon has been used by the Russians for centuries as a flavoring for freshly brewed tea. Its use was introduced to the Western world by Queen Victoria in the late nineteenth century. The revered ruler of Britain discovered the fashionable and tasty flavoring while visiting Vicky, her eldest daughter, who was married to the Prussian king. While lemon complements the taste of scented tea, it also will brighten the flavor of a black tea.

Sugar, honey, and even raspberry jam have been used for centuries to sweeten tea. In Russia, there is an old custom of holding a cube of sugar between your teeth and sucking your tea through it. Honey, the main sweet food of ancient times, is another popular sweetener. While many commercial honeys simply add sweetness to your tea, others will impart additional aroma and flavor. The honey label will usually tell you the type of flower the bees harvested and what flavor you can expect to taste.

storing tea

Although each type of tea has a different shelf life, it's best to use any tea you purchase within six months to a year. Green teas are the most perishable and begin to deteriorate within a year of harvest. Oolong and black teas retain their characteristics for several years.

Keeping the leaves stored in a cool, dry, dark place is the best way to preserve their freshness. Avoid clear glass jars, which expose tea to light. An opaque glass or ceramic container with an airtight lid is best. Another factor contributing to a tea's longevity is the way in which the tea leaf is rolled. Tea leaves rolled into pellets (Gunpowder and Imperial green teas) or twisted (like the black Yunnan) last longer than an open, flat leaf, because less of their surface area is exposed to air. Whatever tea you choose, remember to treat it as you would a delicate spice. Keep it away from heat, moisture, and, of course, other strongly scented teas or spices.

serving tea

. . .

tea customs

Every country serves tea in a manner that expresses its own culture. In China, a cup of tea is a customary way to welcome a guest. In Morocco, shopkeepers still greet prospective customers with a glass of sweet, mint-flavored green tea. In the United Kingdom and Ireland, tea is a welcome pick-me-up at eleven in the morning and four in the afternoon.

In Russia, tea was served with a slice of lemon, a dollop of raspberry jam, or a lump of sugar to be held between the teeth, as a comforting supplement to the one large, daily meal served in traditional Russian households. To make certain that there was a constant supply of freshly brewed tea available, the Russians developed their own way of brewing, using a samovar. The large boiler, or giant kettle, kept water hot all day long. A small teapot filled with tea concentrate rested on its crown, so that a cup of hot tea was available anytime by mixing a small amount of concentrate with hot water.

It was the British or, to be more precise, Anna, the seventh duchess of Bedford, who introduced the delectable custom of afternoon tea to the Western world. The nineteenth-century practice of eating an early breakfast and a late dinner made afternoons long and lean, and Anna solved this dilemma by serving tea with a tantalizing tray of gourmet goodies. Today, this tradition continues to fortify and delight thirty-something power brokers as well as the after-school nursery tea set.

By far the most remarkable tea custom is the Japanese tea ceremony. Known as *Chanoyu,* this ritual has become an important part of Japanese culture since tea was introduced to Japan more than five hundred years ago by Zen monks traveling from China. Once reserved exclusively for men, it is now a ritual that both men and women are welcome to study and share. The Japanese consider the tea ceremony a refuge in which spirit, man, and nature come together, where serenity allows knowledge to become wisdom.

Whether the ceremony takes place in a home or in a separate teahouse, there are guidelines to nurture every aspect, from the selection of guests to the choice of food, utensils, and topics of conversation. The sprinkling of water around a host's entry gate informs guests that preparations are complete and they are welcome to come in. As they remove their coats and shoes, slip into sandals, and walk down the garden path to the teahouse, they leave behind the outside world.

Although different schools of theory govern the ceremony, every gesture by the host and his guests is part of a prescribed ritual. Guided by centuries-old customs, the host or hostess places a small amount of powdered tea, called Matcha, into a tea bowl and, using a bamboo whisk and water, whips it into a light green froth. The tea is reverently poured, offered, and sipped. In this simple and elaborate ceremony, host and guests acknowledge the four principles of an enlightened life—purity, harmony, respect, and tranquillity.

tea implements

As these various traditions suggest, serving tea can be as simple as handing your friend a steaming cup over the breakfast table or as intimidating as taking tea with the queen. Whatever the occasion, there are several implements that will make your task easier. Here is a survey of the basic essentials, with suggestions about how to choose the right one.

teapots

For more than three thousand years, tea drinkers brewed and tasted their tea simply by adding compressed or powdered tea to a kettle or cup. It wasn't until the Ming dynasty (A.D. 1368–1644) that a teapot was considered necessary. As the Chinese began to use dried leaves to make tea, they found that they required a container to hold the steeping concoctions. Wine and water vessels were used for a time, but they often cracked from the heat of the boiling water, and their narrow spouts clogged.

In the early 1500s, in China's Jiangsu province, a potter named Gong Chun created unglazed red and brown stoneware teapots, known as Yixing pots. He used a time-consuming process of drying the clay, pounding it into powder, reconstituting it with cool water, and then drying, pounding, and reconstituting it again to form a smooth clay without any air pockets. This technique enabled the finished teapots to withstand high temperatures and be very durable.

The teapots' unglazed interiors, seasoned with constant use, added new flavor notes with each infusion. Except for their diminutive size—about as big as a woman's clenched fist—these early teapots closely resembled today's teapot. Even the whimsical shapes of fruits and animals that we associate with fashionable boutique dinnerware found their way into the first Asian teapot designs.

To make tea using a Yixing pot, each drinker fills his or her own tiny, hand-molded vessel with tea leaves, replenishing the pot with boiling water after each thimble-sized cupful is poured. Yixing pots continue to be made in the traditional way, and while antique teapots cost thousands of dollars, you can buy a new one on the Internet for around $35 (see "Resources," page 117). By the way, the clay used in the common English Brown Betty teapot is almost identical to that used in the Yixing pots, and although the Brown Betty is glazed, it possesses the same sturdy, heat-retentive qualities.

As tea found its way to seventeenth-century Europe, so did the teapot. Before long, European potters were using domestic clays to imitate Chinese designs. At first, the Dutch tried to adapt their traditional delftware but found that the teapots often broke if they weren't prewarmed.

The British made teapots of sterling, silverplate, or other metals, which solved the breakage problem, but because metal is a superb heat conductor, did not keep the tea hot for long. (We've all met those odious metal teapots with café counter tea.) In 1693, the discovery in Staffordshire, England, of a clay suitable for making delicate and heat-resistant stoneware solved a practical problem, but the results were not aesthetic. What European tea drinkers desired was the delicate yet hardy Chinese porcelain first described to them by Marco Polo in 1477. It was not until early in the eighteenth century that the British discovered the materials and techniques required to reproduce the fine Chinese porcelains they so admired.

In the last four hundred years, the design and function of teapots has changed very little. The same principles apply to a priceless Ming teapot as to your favorite worn and chipped china pot. When buying a teapot, make sure the lid is secure and won't fall off when you pour. (It wasn't until the nineteenth century that someone wisely manufactured a lid with a small protrusion, or tongue, to slip under the pot's lip.) Check out the teapot's spout, and, if possible, try it out. There's nothing more maddening than a drippy spout. Hold the pot by its handle to see if it feels right in your hand. There should be enough room between your fingers and the handle so that your knuckles don't get pinched.

With a multitude of teapots from which to choose, from automatic models to teapots with built-in infusers, take the time to see which one best suits your needs and your personality. And while you're at it, check out the tea cozy. These padded covers come in any number of patterns and shapes and help insulate the teapot and keep its contents hot.

teacups

Teacups were originally tea bowls, much like the ones you might find in an Asian restaurant today. Eighth-century Chinese writer Lu Yu describes the tea bowl in great detail, down to the glaze that looks best with a particular tea. He was fond of a blue glaze that turned red tea jade green. (Today, green tea enthusiasts still favor white or celadon cups for highlighting the slight differences in green teas' various hues.) The Japanese further adapted the bowl's design to reflect different seasons and aspects of their elaborate tea ceremonies.

In eighteenth-century England, British tea drinkers were enchanted with the shallow, handleless cups used to serve Asian tea, but it wasn't long before hot fingertips and the affordable price of tea convinced people to switch to a larger, handled version. Following the fashion of those drinking coffee and possets (a warm alcoholic drink made with milk), tea drinkers adopted a single-handled cup version, letting the double handle remain with hot chocolate enthusiasts. Choosing your own teacup is a matter of personal taste. The most important thing is that it feels good in your hand and is pleasing to your eye.

teakettles

While you can boil your water in any saucepan or soup pot, a teakettle is a handy investment. Most kettles are made out of metal, and the best have a chromium-plated copper body. The same principles you use in choosing a teapot apply to the choice of a kettle. My favorite everyday kettle is a Russell Hobbs. Automatic and electric, this sturdy brand can go anywhere there is an electrical outlet. I keep mine on the small table next to my computer.

infusers and strainers

When you use a tea bag, the intricate world of tea infusers and strainers is lost to you. To some, this may be a relief, but I find an infuser part of the reassuring ritual of tea.

A tea infuser is a perforated receptacle in which a measured amount of loose tea is placed. Known as a tea egg or ball, this metal container is placed in the teapot before the boiling water is added. It's important not to fill your infuser too full. Half full is best, because the leaves need room to expand as they absorb water. If you do decide to make a large amount of tea, don't overstuff your egg; instead, use two. If you are using loose tea or a teapot with a built-in infuser instead of a tea ball, a tea strainer will come in handy to catch stragglers and give you a clear cup of tea.

• • •

Many foods have been created as traditional complements to tea. In the following chapters, you will find recipes to accompany your tea, whether it's hot, iced, spiced, or spiked. You also will find sweet and savory recipes that use tea as an essential ingredient. And, for a pause that refreshes, there are recipes for making a tempting array of delicious tea drinks.

recipes

beverages

. . .

the perfect iced tea

Serves 4

Black tea is the classic foundation for iced tea, but try experimenting with blended and flavored teas, green teas, and herbals. ❖ Here are two methods for making sure your iced tea is perfect every time. When you brew iced tea in the traditional manner, with hot water, the tea will often become cloudy when chilled. If this happens, add a little boiling water to the chilled tea and give it a stir. If you want your chilled tea to be crystal clear, use the cold-water method. For iced tea to be the same strength from start to finish, use ice cubes made from leftover tea.

4   CUPS (1 QUART) COLD WATER

¼   CUP LOOSE BLACK TEA LEAVES,
     OR 4 TEA BAGS

ICE CUBES

SUGAR SYRUP FOR SWEETENING
     (RECIPE FOLLOWS; OPTIONAL)

¼   CUP LOOSE BLACK TEA LEAVES,
     OR 4 TEA BAGS

4   CUPS (1 QUART) COLD WATER

ICE CUBES

hot-water method

In a saucepan, bring 2 cups of the cold water to a boil. Remove from the heat and add the tea leaves. Stir, cover, and let steep for 5 minutes. Stir and strain the mixture through a fine sieve to remove the tea leaves. (For crystal-clear tea, strain a second time through filter paper—the kind used to make drip coffee.) Pour the strained tea into a pitcher containing the remaining 2 cups of cold water. Stir, and pour into tall glasses filled with ice cubes. Sweeten with Sugar Syrup if desired.

cold-water method

Fill a large glass container with the tea and cold water. Stir well and chill overnight.

If you used loose tea, strain the mixture through a fine sieve to remove the tea leaves. (For crystal-clear tea, strain a second time through filter paper—the kind used to make drip coffee.) Refrigerate until serving time. Stir, and pour into tall glasses filled with ice cubes. Sweeten with Sugar Syrup if desired.

sugar syrup: In a small saucepan, combine 2 cups water and 2 cups sugar. Bring the mixture to a boil over medium heat. Simmer until clear, about 10 minutes. Remove from the heat and let cool to room temperature. Store indefinitely in a covered container in the refrigerator. Use in iced tea according to taste.

lemon sugar syrup: Follow the recipe for Sugar Syrup, stirring in the zest of 3 small lemons, peeled in strips, after the mixture reaches a boil. Proceed as directed, straining and discarding the zest after the liquid has cooled.

amanda's blend

**Makes a bit more than 3/4 pound,
or between 150 and 170 cups**

Blending your own signature tea is easy to do, especially when there are several complementary teas and tea blends that you like. My friend Amanda Baines Ashley mixes her three favorites to make this blend. Those of us lucky enough to be in her office at four o'clock get treated to a cup of her brisk and delightful tea. I like it best with milk and sugar.

½ POUND LOOSE ENGLISH BREAKFAST TEA

¼ POUND LOOSE DARJEELING TEA

⅛ POUND LOOSE EARL GREY TEA

Place the loose tea leaves in a large mixing bowl and stir until well blended. Store in a clean, opaque glass or ceramic jar with a screwtop lid or tight-fitting cork. Give the jar a good shake to help distribute the different ingredients before removing any tea for brewing. To use, measure 1 rounded teaspoon for each 6-ounce cup of freshly boiled water. Steep for 3 to 5 minutes.

my chai tea

Serves 1

Preparing a single cup of chai is as easy as raiding your spice cabinet. Here is my current favorite recipe. One of the pleasures of chai is changing the spice mix according to the season and your mood. Feel free to add or delete the spices and adjust the sweetness.

½ CUP MILK

½ CUP WATER

1   ROUNDED TEASPOON ASSAM, KEEMUN,
     OR OTHER BLACK TEA LEAVES, OR
     1 TEA BAG

1   ROUNDED TEASPOON MY CHAI TEA
     SPICE MIX (RECIPE FOLLOWS)

1   TO 2 TEASPOONS SUGAR

In a small saucepan, combine the milk and water. Over medium heat, bring to a boil. Reduce the heat to low and stir in the tea and chai spice mix. Remove from the heat, cover, and steep for 5 minutes. Strain into a prewarmed mug and stir in the sugar to taste.

my chai tea spice mix: In a cup or small bowl, blend together 1 tablespoon ground cardamom, 1 tablespoon ground cinnamon, 2 teaspoons ground ginger, 2 teaspoons ground cloves, and 1 teaspoon ground black pepper. Store in a clean, opaque glass or ceramic jar with a screwtop lid or tight-fitting cork. Give the jar a good shake to help distribute the different ingredients before removing the spice mix for brewing. Makes a scant ¼ cup.

leapin' lizards chai tea

Serves 2

My friend Kathlyn Meskel says the name of her chai comes from her reaction the first time she savored a sip of this brew. I think you'll agree: it's got flavor and packs a kick.

3/4 CUP MILK

3/4 CUP WATER

2 ROUNDED TEASPOONS LEAPIN' LIZARDS CHAI TEA BLEND (RECIPE FOLLOWS)

2 TO 3 TEASPOONS SUGAR

In a small saucepan, combine the milk and water. Over medium heat, bring to a boil. Reduce the heat to low and stir in the chai tea blend. Remove from the heat, cover, and steep for 5 minutes. Strain into a prewarmed teapot or pitcher, and stir in the sugar.

leapin' lizards chai tea blend: With a mortar and pestle or a meat tenderizer, coarsely grind, crush, or crumble 2 tablespoons green cardamom seeds, 1 tablespoon whole cloves, 1 tablespoon whole black peppercorns, and one 4-inch cinnamon stick coarsely chopped. In a quart-sized plastic bag, place the spice mixture and 1 cup of loose black tea leaves. Blow into the bag as if blowing up a balloon. Once it's inflated, hold the bag shut and shake until the ingredients are well combined. Store in a clean, opaque glass or ceramic jar with a screwtop lid or tight-fitting cork. Give the jar a good shake to help distribute the different ingredients before removing any tea for brewing. Makes 1 cup dried tea blend, or 48 servings.

green tea chai blend: Follow the recipe for Leapin' Lizards Chai Tea Blend, substituting a green tea such as a Sencha for the black tea. Proceed as directed.

rest and refresh tea

Makes about 1 cup, or about 12 servings

This herbal tea blend makes a flavorful afternoon pick-me-up. The chamomile has a restful quality and its taste is applelike, while the basil and citrus peels refresh with their peppery zing.

½ CUP DRIED CHAMOMILE FLOWERS

¼ CUP DRIED BASIL LEAVES

2 TABLESPOONS DRIED PEPPERMINT LEAVES

2 TABLESPOONS DRIED LEMON PEEL

2 TABLESPOONS DRIED ORANGE PEEL

Place all of the ingredients in a quart-sized plastic bag. Blow into the bag as if blowing up a balloon. Once it's inflated, hold the bag shut and shake until well combined. Store in a clean, opaque glass or ceramic jar with a screwtop lid or tight-fitting cork. Give the jar a good shake to help distribute the different ingredients before removing any tea for brewing.

To use, measure 1 rounded teaspoon for each 6- to 8-ounce cup of freshly boiled water. Steep for 5 to 6 minutes.

eye-opening tea: For a gentle yet brisk morning brew, follow the recipe for Rest and Refresh Tea, using ½ cup green tea, ¼ cup dried ginger root (available at natural food and herbal tea stores), one 4-inch cinnamon stick, coarsely chopped, and 2 tablespoons dried peppermint leaves or dried rosemary leaves. To use, measure 2 teaspoons for each 6- to 8-ounce cup of hot yet not simmering water. Steep for 3 to 5 minutes.

wild women's tea: For some razzmatazz at the next girls' night out, follow the Rest and Refresh recipe, using ½ cup Assam, Sri Lanka (Ceylon), or other black tea, ¼ cup dried lavender flowers, 2 tablespoons dried rosemary leaves, and 2 tablespoons dried lemon balm leaves (optional). To use, measure 2 teaspoons for each 6- to 8-ounce cup of hot yet not simmering water. Steep for 3 to 5 minutes. Sweeten with a chunk of crystallized ginger.

catalina citrus sun tea

Serves 6 to 8

The first time I tasted sun tea was on California's Catalina Island when my dad and mom took my brother and me there in an old Chris Craft wooden cruiser. Mom set a pitcher of water with several tea bags out on the shellacked deck, and within a few hours the clear water was a Lipton-tea brown. Swirling the bags, squeezing oranges and a lemon, adding lots of sugar and chips of ice from the ice chest, she made the most delicious iced juice tea. I add mint, and I brew it on a sunny windowsill. Each time I do, I remember being a kid again.

1/2 TO 3/4 CUP BLACK TEA LEAVES, OR 9 TO 12 TEA BAGS

4   CUPS (1 QUART) COLD WATER

3   TABLESPOONS SUGAR

1   SIX-INCH SPRIG OF FRESH MINT

2   CUPS FRESH ORANGE JUICE

JUICE OF 1 LEMON

1   PEELED (WITH MEMBRANE REMOVED) AND SEEDED ORANGE, CUT INTO THIN PIECES

ORANGE SLICES AND MINT LEAVES, FOR GARNISH

In a glass jar, combine the tea, water, sugar, and mint. Screw on the cap and shake gently. Place the jar in a warm, sunny location for 3 hours.

Blend the orange juice and lemon juice into the tea mixture. If desired, strain the mixture through a sieve. Add the orange pieces and refrigerate for several hours. Garnish with orange slices and mint leaves.

early mint sun tea: For a quick, thirst-quenching sun tea, replace the black tea with 2 tablespoons Earl Grey tea in the recipe for Catalina Citrus Sun Tea, and omit the orange and lemon juice. Proceed as directed.

raspberry fizz: Follow the recipe for Catalina Citrus Sun Tea. Place 1 to 2 tablespoons raspberry syrup in a 10-ounce glass. Fill the glass 1/3 to 1/2 full of the chilled tea, and top with your favorite sparkling water. For a subtler taste, you can omit the syrup and add your favorite raspberry-flavored sparkling water. Garnish with a wooden skewer threaded with the tip of a mint sprig and fresh raspberries.

hollywood spritzer: Follow the recipe for Catalina Citrus Sun Tea. Place 1 tablespoon Cointreau in the bottom of a chilled glass or champagne flute. Fill the glass 1/2 full of chilled tea and top with an inexpensive champagne.

green tea margarita

Serves 1

When summer's on the way, Margarita comes to stay, and there's more than one way to shake her. She can be a party-in-a-glass or an elegant companion. In this recipe, she's all dressed up and blended with green chai ice cubes. With a hint of spice in each sip, she's a seductive señorita.

For each drink, you will need:

1 LIME OR LEMON WEDGE

SAUCER OF SUGAR FOR COATING RIM
   OF GLASS

1/2 TO 2/3 CUP STRONGLY BREWED GREEN
   TEA CHAI (PAGE 70), FROZEN INTO 6
   TO 8 SMALL ICE CUBES

2 1/2 TABLESPOONS (1 1/4 OUNCES) PREMIUM
   TEQUILA

1 TABLESPOON FRESH LEMON JUICE

1 TABLESPOON COINTREAU

2 TEASPOONS SUGAR

Rub the lime wedge around the rim of an old-fashioned glass. Dip and rotate the rim in the saucer of sugar, making sure to keep the sugar on the outside. In a blender, combine the chai ice cubes, tequila, lemon juice, Cointreau, and sugar. Blend on the pulse setting until slushy. Pour into the sugar-rimmed glass.

variation: For those who prefer their libations over ice, fill a sugar-rimmed old-fashioned glass 1/3 full of chai ice cubes. Follow the recipe for Green Tea Margarita, using the blender's pulse feature to blend the ingredients until the ice is coarsely chopped and the mixture is frothy. Strain the mixture through a bar strainer into the prepared glass.

centennial cheer

When the smooth and smoky flavor of Lapsang Souchong gets together with Irish whiskey, it's a powerful brew, perfect for warming your insides after a great day of skiing or a chilly day at work.

4 TEASPOONS SUGAR

4 STRIPS LEMON ZEST, EACH STUCK WITH
  1 WHOLE CLOVE

4 CINNAMON STICKS (OPTIONAL)

¼ CUP BOURBON OR IRISH WHISKEY

2 CUPS FRESHLY PREPARED HOT LAPSANG
  SOUCHONG TEA

Warm 4 small mugs or glasses with hot water. Place 1 teaspoon sugar, 1 lemon zest strip, 1 cinnamon stick (if desired), and 1 tablespoon bourbon in each mug. Pour ½ cup tea into each mug and stir.

baked goods
and cookies

. . .

saucer scones

Makes about 1 dozen scones

Small enough to place on a teacup saucer, these bite-sized cream scones are the quintessential teatime treat. They're ideal for dipping. Try pairing them with a small dipping bowl filled with chilled lemon yogurt and another filled with homemade strawberry sauce or slightly warmed strawberry jam.

1   CUP BLEACHED ALL-PURPOSE FLOUR

2   TEASPOONS SUGAR

2   TEASPOONS BAKING POWDER

1/4 TEASPOON SALT

1/2 CUP PLUS 2 TABLESPOONS HEAVY
    WHIPPING CREAM

glaze

1   EGG, LIGHTLY BEATEN

1/4 CUP MILK

Preheat the oven to 425°F. Line a baking sheet with parchment paper or grease it.

In a medium bowl, whisk the flour, sugar, baking powder, and salt together. Make a well in the center of the flour and add the heavy cream. Stir with a wooden spoon until the mixture just forms a dough. Don't overbeat or the scones will be heavy.

Dust hands with flour and knead the dough gently on a lightly floured surface several times. Roll out the dough 1/4 inch thick. Dip a 2-inch round biscuit cutter into flour, shake off the excess, and push straight down to cut the dough. (If you twist the cutter, chances are the scones will not rise properly.) Place scones on the baking sheet.

In a small bowl, mix the egg and milk together for the glaze, and brush over the top of each scone. Bake until golden brown, about 12 minutes.

traditional tea scones: Follow the recipe for Saucer Scones, but instead of rolling out the dough, shape it into an 8-inch circle. With a sharp knife, cut the dough into 8 wedges. Place on the baking sheet and bake until golden brown, about 12 minutes.

golden triangle tea scones: Follow the recipe for Traditional Tea Scones, adding 1/4 cup whole or coarsely chopped cranberries, 1/4 cup whole or coarsely chopped golden raisins, and 1 teaspoon grated orange zest to the flour mixture. Proceed as directed, cutting the dough into 8 wedges.

savory scone biscuits: Follow the recipe for Saucer Scones, decreasing the sugar to 1 teaspoon and adding 2 tablespoons finely grated Parmesan cheese and 1 tablespoon finely minced chives to the flour mixture. Proceed as directed.

ginger-spice tea cake

Makes one 9-inch cake; serves 6 to 8

If you're wondering what to make for an afternoon treat or a simple supper dessert, this surprisingly easy and handsome cake, with its glistening shards of crystallized ginger, is the delicious answer. And on weekends, your family will revel in the aroma of this chai-spice breakfast cake baking in the oven. They'll rise and shine for a sliver or a slice, especially when it's served with a brisk and bracing pot of your favorite breakfast blend of black tea.

1½ CUPS BLEACHED ALL-PURPOSE FLOUR

2 TEASPOONS BAKING POWDER

½ TEASPOON BAKING SODA

½ TEASPOON SALT

1 TEASPOON GROUND CARDAMOM

1 TEASPOON GROUND GINGER

½ TO 1 TEASPOON GROUND WHITE PEPPER

1 CUP SOUR CREAM AT ROOM TEMPERATURE

2 EGGS AT ROOM TEMPERATURE

½ CUP FIRMLY PACKED LIGHT BROWN SUGAR

½ CUP PLUS 2 TABLESPOONS GRANULATED SUGAR

2 TEASPOONS VANILLA EXTRACT

⅓ TO ½ CUP FRUIT PRESERVES AT ROOM TEMPERATURE

⅓ CUP THINLY SLICED CRYSTALLIZED GINGER

Preheat the oven to 350°F. Lightly grease and flour the bottom and sides of a 9-inch round cake pan.

In a large bowl, whisk the flour, baking powder, baking soda, salt, cardamom, ginger, and white pepper together. Set aside.

In a medium bowl, whisk the sour cream and eggs together until blended. Beat in the brown sugar, ½ cup granulated sugar, and vanilla. Stir the egg mixture into the flour mixture until just blended. Do not overbeat. Spread ¾ of the batter into the prepared pan. With the back of a spoon, lightly spread the preserves over the batter. Spread the remaining batter evenly over the preserves. (Don't worry if a swirl of preserve shows through.) Lay the ginger slices over the top of the cake, leaving a 1-inch rim around the outside edge. Sprinkle the top with the remaining 2 tablespoons granulated sugar. Bake until the top is brown all over and the cake pulls away from the sides of the pan, 35 to 40 minutes. Transfer to a wire rack to cool for 20 to 30 minutes before slicing.

nursery cakes with sweet cream and strawberry jam

Makes 20 cakes

These sweet and irresistible bite-sized butter cakes began as a treat for my daughter Julie's teddy bear tea parties. Now they're a family favorite for just about any event, including grown-up teas, backyard picnics, or an all-out formal occasion. You'll find the recipe is quick, as it is based on a simple sheet cake.

1   CUP BLEACHED ALL-PURPOSE FLOUR

1   TEASPOON BAKING SODA

½ TEASPOON SALT

¼ CUP UNSALTED BUTTER AT ROOM TEMPERATURE

¾ CUP SUGAR

1   EGG AT ROOM TEMPERATURE

1   TEASPOON VANILLA EXTRACT

½ CUP MILK AT ROOM TEMPERATURE

SCANT ½ CUP STRAWBERRY OR RED CURRANT PRESERVES

⅔ CUP LIGHTLY SWEETENED WHIPPED CREAM

TINY EDIBLE FLOWERS SUCH AS VIOLETS, OR HERB LEAVES, FOR GARNISH (OPTIONAL)

Preheat the oven to 400°F. Lightly grease a 9-by-13-by-2-inch baking pan.

In a bowl, whisk the flour, baking soda, and salt together. In a mixing bowl, using an electric mixer on low, combine the butter and sugar until crumbly. Add the egg and vanilla, and continue to beat until the mixture is smooth and creamy. Beat in the milk. (The mixture will look curdy.) On low speed, gradually add the flour mixture and mix until well blended. Pour the batter into the pan and, with a spatula, gently spread it over the bottom of the pan to form a thin layer. Bake until golden brown all over, 12 to 15 minutes.

Transfer the pan to a wire rack to cool, 15 to 20 minutes. Use a 2-inch round cookie or garnish cutter to cut out 20 circles in the sheet cake. Remove the nursery cakes with a thin-bladed spatula.

To serve, spread the top of each cake with 1 teaspoon of preserves and top with a dollop of whipped cream, or place a dollop of preserves and a dollop of whipped cream on top of each cake. Garnish with a flower or leaf, if desired.

variation: For a simple finish, omit the preserves and whipped cream and sift powdered sugar over the entire sheet cake before cutting out the circles.

lemon oatmeal crisps

Makes about 2 dozen cookies

During a visit to the Portland Art Museum, I was treated to one of these butter-crisp cookies by museum volunteer Myrthle Griffin. I don't remember the exhibit, but I'll never forget the cookie. When afternoon tea includes a cookie, this is the one to have. The lemony flavor is delicious with a brisk cup of freshly brewed Assam or Darjeeling. These cookies are also terrific as lunch box treats.

½ CUP UNBLEACHED OR BLEACHED ALL-PURPOSE FLOUR

¼ TEASPOON BAKING SODA

¼ TEASPOON SALT

½ CUP (1 STICK) UNSALTED BUTTER

½ CUP SUGAR

½ TEASPOON LEMON EXTRACT

½ TEASPOON MINCED LEMON ZEST

¾ CUP OLD-FASHIONED ROLLED OATS

Preheat the oven to 350°F. Line two baking sheets with parchment paper, or leave them ungreased.

In a small bowl, whisk the flour, baking soda, and salt together.

In a large bowl, combine the butter and sugar. Using an electric mixer on medium speed, beat until very light and fluffy, 10 minutes. (That's right: 10 minutes.) Beat in the lemon extract and zest. With the mixer on low, beat in the flour mixture. Beat in the oats until blended. The dough will be soft.

Drop by rounded teaspoonfuls onto a baking sheet, leaving at least 1½ inches between the mounds of dough. Bake until lightly golden, 13 to 15 minutes. Cool slightly on the baking sheet before transferring to a wire rack to cool completely. Store in an airtight container.

paradise chocolate chip cookies: Follow the recipe for Lemon Oatmeal Crisps, adding ½ cup white chocolate chips and ½ cup coarsely chopped macadamia nuts to the batter. Proceed as directed.

cashew shortbread

Makes 1 dozen cookies

What's afternoon tea without a wedge of shortbread? In this recipe, cashews give the buttery cookie a delicate scent and a lovely, unexpected taste. For purists who love a traditional shortbread, simply eliminate the nuts. ✣ I like to grate frozen butter into the dry ingredients for a flakier cookie. It isn't traditional, but it sure works.

1   CUP SALTED CASHEWS, FINELY CHOPPED
(SEE NOTE)

1   CUP BLEACHED ALL-PURPOSE FLOUR

1   SCANT CUP POWDERED SUGAR

1/4 CUP CORNSTARCH

2 1/2 TEASPOONS GROUND GINGER

3/4 CUP (1 1/2 STICKS) COLD UNSALTED BUTTER

1   TO 2 TEASPOONS GRANULATED SUGAR

Preheat the oven to 325°F. Have ready a 9-inch round cake pan with a removable bottom, or line the bottom of a 9-inch round cake pan with a round of parchment paper.

In a medium bowl, whisk the cashews, flour, powdered sugar, cornstarch, and ginger together. Using the large holes of a flat or four-sided grater, grate the butter into the flour mixture. With your fingertips, work the mixture together until it is crumbly and the butter begins to soften. Continue to work until the dough can be packed into a ball.

Pat the mixture into the prepared pan. Press to an even thickness, covering the bottom of the pan. Pierce the dough all over with a fork. Bake until golden, about 35 minutes. Immediately sprinkle the granulated sugar over the surface. Use a sharp knife to cut into 12 wedges. Let cool in the pan for 15 minutes. Unmold and transfer to a wire rack to cool completely. Store in an airtight container.

note: For finely chopped cashews, use a small food chopper, blender, or food processor. Process the nuts with several on-off bursts for 20 seconds.

white chocolate cashew shortbread: Prepare Cashew Shortbread and let cool. Melt 2 ounces white chocolate in a double boiler over barely simmering water. Dust the crumbs from each cookie with a pastry brush and dip the curved edge of each cookie into the melted chocolate. Sprinkle with additional chopped cashews if desired.

tea straws with lemon curd and candied ginger

Makes 1 dozen straws

They're dazzling to look at and even better to eat. These slender, flaky pastries make a spectacular centerpiece when grouped together in a mint julep cup or a small, decorative vase. Once you take your first bite, there's a surprise in store: the buttery, crisp pastry reveals a tart lemon curd filling with flecks of crystallized ginger. ✤ With help from the freezer section of your supermarket, the phyllo sheets are easy to buy.

THREE 17-BY-12-INCH PHYLLO SHEETS, THAWED

½ CUP (1 STICK) MELTED BUTTER

¼ CUP PURCHASED OR HOMEMADE LEMON CURD

¼ CUP FINELY CHOPPED CRYSTALLIZED GINGER

Place an oven rack in the upper third of the oven. Preheat the oven to 375°F. Line a baking sheet with parchment paper.

Unfold the phyllo sheets so that they lie flat. Cut them in half crosswise to form 6 sheets. To prevent drying out, cover with waxed paper and a damp towel. Remove sheet and place it in front of you on a work surface, with the longest side facing you. Lightly brush the lower half with butter. Spoon and spread 2 teaspoons lemon curd lengthwise across the center of the sheet. Sprinkle the curd with 2 teaspoons chopped crystallized ginger. Fold the phyllo almost in half lengthwise, leaving a 1-inch rim. Brush lightly with butter, up to and including the edge. Starting with the side closest to you, roll up the phyllo tightly to form a 12-inch straw. Transfer to the baking sheet, seam side down. Repeat to make 5 more straws.

Bake until golden, 12 to 14 minutes. Transfer to a wire rack to cool. To serve, break each straw in half. Store in an airtight container.

chunky chocolate and candied ginger straws: Follow the recipe for Tea Straws with Lemon Curd and Candied Ginger, substituting ⅓ cup white chocolate chips for the lemon curd. For each straw, sprinkle 1 scant tablespoon of the chips over the phyllo.

sweet spice straws: In a small bowl or cup, combine ½ teaspoon ground cardamom, ¼ teaspoon ground cinnamon, ¼ teaspoon ground ginger, and a pinch of ground cloves. Follow the recipe for Tea Straws with Lemon Curd and Candied Ginger, substituting the spice mixture for the lemon curd and crystallized ginger. Use 1 tablespoon of the spice mixture for each straw.

chocolate coco wafers

Makes about 3 dozen cookies

If rolling out thin dough is not your idea of fun, roll the dough to a thickness comfortable for your level of skill and make a soft, buttery chocolate cookie instead of a thin, crisp one.

1 OUNCE (1 SQUARE) SEMISWEET CHOCOLATE

1 CUP BLEACHED OR UNBLEACHED ALL-PURPOSE FLOUR

1/4 CUP UNSWEETENED DUTCH-PROCESS COCOA POWDER

1/2 TEASPOON BAKING POWDER

1/4 TEASPOON GROUND CINNAMON

PINCH OF SALT

1/4 CUP UNSALTED BUTTER

1/2 CUP SUGAR

1 EGG

1 1/2 OUNCES MELTED SEMISWEET CHOCOLATE FOR DECORATING (OPTIONAL)

In a double boiler over simmering water, or in the microwave, melt the chocolate and set aside to cool slightly.

In a small bowl, whisk the flour, cocoa, baking powder, cinnamon, and salt together.

In a large bowl, combine the butter and sugar. Using an electric mixer on medium speed, beat until light and fluffy, at least 5 minutes. Beat in the egg. Slowly beat in the melted chocolate until well blended. With the mixer on low, beat in the flour mixture. The dough will be sticky. With floured hands, gather the dough and pat it into a disk. Cover in plastic wrap and chill for 2 hours.

Preheat the oven to 350°F. Line two baking sheets with parchment paper, or leave them ungreased.

On a lightly floured board, or on a pastry cloth, or between 2 sheets of heavy-duty plastic wrap, roll the dough out 1/8 inch thick. (If the dough is too hard, leave it at room temperature for 5 to 10 minutes.) Lightly dip a round cookie cutter in flour (this makes it easier to release the cookie), and press it straight down into the dough.

Use a spatula to place the cookies 1/2 inch apart on the baking sheet. Bake until set, 9 to 10 minutes. Cool slightly on the baking sheet before transferring to a wire rack to cool completely. Store in an airtight container.

If you wish to decorate the cookies, spread waxed paper under the wire racks to catch the drips. Using the tines of a fork or a plastic bag with a small hole cut in one corner, drizzle or pipe the melted chocolate over the cookies and let set.

variation: For softer, thicker cookies, roll the chilled dough to 1/4 inch thickness, and proceed as directed, and increase baking time until cookies are set.

desserts

...

blackberry and lime curd tartlets

Makes six 4-inch tartlets

Tea and tartlets—what could be more civilized or more delicious? In this recipe, the tartlets use two luscious curds, blackberry and lime. You can spoon or pipe the curds into the pastry shells side by side or in large, distinctive patterns. Either way, they give a delectable impression of two distinctive but complementary flavors.

blackberry curd

1½ CUPS FRESH OR FROZEN BLACKBERRIES

2 TABLESPOONS SUGAR

¼ CUP BUTTER

3 EGG YOLKS

lime curd

¼ CUP FRESH LIME JUICE (ABOUT 2 LARGE LIMES)

½ CUP SUGAR

¼ CUP BUTTER

3 EGG YOLKS

2 TO 3 TEASPOONS LIME ZEST

pâte sucrée

1¼ CUPS UNBLEACHED ALL-PURPOSE FLOUR

3 TABLESPOONS SUGAR

½ CUP (1 STICK) COLD UNSALTED BUTTER

1 EGG YOLK

1 TO 2 TABLESPOONS ICE WATER

garnishes

BLACKBERRIES

EDIBLE PURPLE FLOWERS SUCH AS PANSIES OR VIOLETS

TINY MINT LEAVES

to make the blackberry curd: Heat the berries in a saucepan over medium heat to break them down, 5 to 7 minutes. Pass the berries and juice through a fine sieve to remove the seeds. You should have about ½ cup of purée. Combine the purée, sugar, butter, and egg yolks in the top of a double boiler over simmering water. Whisk constantly until the mixture thickens, about 5 minutes. Remove from the heat and whisk for another 1 to 2 minutes as the mixture thickens and cools. Strain into a container. Cover the top of the curd with plastic wrap so that no skin forms. Cool completely and chill until ready to use, or up to 3 days. You should have about 3/4 cup.

to make the lime curd: Heat the lime juice, sugar, butter, and egg yolks in the top of a double boiler over simmering water. Whisk constantly until the mixture thickens, about 10 minutes. Remove from the heat and whisk for another 1 to 2 minutes as the mixture thickens and cools. Strain into a container and stir in the lime zest. Cover the top of the curd with plastic wrap so that no skin forms. Cool completely and chill for 6 hours or overnight. The consistency will be thick and creamy. It can be stored for up to 3 days. You should have about 3/4 cup.

to make the pastry: Combine the flour and sugar in the bowl of a food processor. Add the butter and process with on-off bursts until the mixture looks like coarse meal. Add the egg yolk. With the machine running, add the ice water, 1 tablespoon at a time, until the dough collects into a mass on the blade. Turn out onto a piece of plastic wrap. Flatten into a disc and wrap. Chill for 1 hour.

(continued)

to make the tartlets: Preheat the oven to 400°F. Spray six 4-inch tartlet pans with cooking spray. Roll out the dough, cut, and press into the pans. Trim the edges with a knife. Refrigerate the shells for 30 to 45 minutes. Prick the bottoms with a fork. Line the shells with parchment paper and fill with dried beans or pie weights. Transfer to a baking sheet and bake until the edges are light brown, about 15 minutes. Remove the paper and beans and continue to bake until golden brown, about 10 minutes. Transfer to a wire rack and cool completely.

to assemble the tartlets: Use a pastry bag, or spoon the two curds into the baked tart shells, either side by side or in patterns. Garnish with berries, flowers, and/or mint.

summer chai-spice pavlova

Serves 4

Named after the Russian ballerina Anna Pavlova, this exuberant combination of meringue, fresh fruit, and whipping cream takes on the personality of the cook who creates it. I've added chai spice to the meringue, which delicately accents each ingredient. You can use the fruits I've suggested or your own backyard bounty.

chai meringues

3/4 CUP GRANULATED SUGAR

1/4 TEASPOON CHINESE FIVE-SPICE POWDER

1/2 TEASPOON GROUND CARDAMOM

1/4 TEASPOON GROUND GINGER

3 EGG WHITES

3/8 TEASPOON CREAM OF TARTAR

orange honey sauce

1 CUP FRESH ORANGE JUICE

1/2 CUP HONEY

2 TEASPOONS GRATED ORANGE ZEST

2 1/2 CUPS LIGHTLY SWEETENED
WHIPPED CREAM

2 TO 3 CUPS SLICED FRESH FRUIT, SUCH
AS NECTARINES AND BLUEBERRIES OR
A MEDLEY OF FRESH BERRIES

POWDERED SUGAR FOR DUSTING

EDIBLE FLOWERS AND MINT LEAVES,
FOR GARNISH

to make the meringues: Preheat the oven to 200°F. Line a baking sheet with parchment paper. Draw four 4-inch circles on the paper, leaving at least 1 inch between them. In a small bowl, whisk together the sugar, five-spice powder, cardamom, and ginger. Set aside. In the bowl of a standing mixer fitted with a whisk, beat the egg whites and cream of tartar on medium-low speed until frothy, about 1 1/2 minutes. Increase the speed to medium-high, and slowly add the sugar mixture, whisking until stiff, about 2 1/2 minutes. Increase the speed to high, and continue to whisk until stiff and glossy, about 4 minutes.

Spoon about 1/3 cup of meringue onto the prepared parchment paper circles, making an indentation in the top of each mound with the back of a spoon. Any leftover meringue can be made into individual meringue kisses. Bake for 2 to 2 1/2 hours, or until dry throughout. If further drying is needed, turn off the oven and leave them inside, for 30 to 90 minutes. Transfer to wire racks to cool. Store in an airtight container for up to 2 weeks.

to make the sauce: In a saucepan, combine the orange juice and honey and bring to a simmer over medium heat. Continue to cook, stirring constantly with a wooden spoon, until the mixture is reduced by half. Remove from the heat. Strain the mixture and stir in the orange zest. Cool and chill until ready to use. Makes 3/4 cup. To serve, place a meringue shell on a plate. Spoon a scant 1/2 cup whipped cream on top of the shell. Spoon the fruit topping over the cream. Decorate with a dollop of whipped cream. Drizzle with 2 to 2 1/2 tablespoons of the sauce. Dust with powdered sugar and garnish with edible flowers and mint.

moroccan mint granita

Reminiscent of the traditional sweet tea served after a North African meal, this bracing granita is made with green tea and mint. Wonderful when the weather is hot, it's a refreshing afternoon delight and a surprising palate cleanser, as well as a delicious dessert.

2   CUPS WATER

1½ TEASPOONS GUNPOWDER OR PEARL
    DEW GREEN TEA LEAVES

¼   CUP PLUS 2 TABLESPOONS CHOPPED
    FRESH MINT LEAVES

¼   CUP PLUS 2 TABLESPOONS SUGAR

MINT LEAVES, FOR GARNISH

In a saucepan, bring the water to a boil. Add the tea and mint leaves. Cover and let steep for 5 minutes. Strain into another container, and blend in the sugar to taste. The flavor should be quite sweet. Let cool to room temperature.

Pour the tea mixture into a 9-by-5-inch loaf pan and place it in the freezer. After 30 minutes, remove the pan from the freezer and stir to break up the ice crystals. Return to the freezer. Repeat the process every 30 minutes over a period of 1½ to 2 hours, until the ice acquires a firm, smooth consistency.

To serve, scoop into glasses or demitasse cups and garnish with mint leaves. For best flavor, serve the granita the same day you make it.

tea cream with cardamom

Serves 6

Tea is not often thought of as a flavoring for food, but it can add a subtle touch to many dishes. As an unusual finale to your next dinner party, try serving this simple-to-make tea cream in your favorite set of demitasse cups. The enticing taste of tea with cardamom is mystifying. You'll find guests wanting "just one more bite" to figure out what tastes so good.

1   CUP HEAVY WHIPPING CREAM

3   TABLESPOONS ENGLISH BREAKFAST OR
    DARJEELING TEA LEAVES

4   GREEN CARDAMOM PODS, CRUSHED

1/3 CUP SUGAR

PINCH OF SALT

1 1/2 TEASPOONS UNFLAVORED GELATIN

1 1/2 CUPS SOUR CREAM

ORANGE HONEY SAUCE (SEE PAGE 93)

JULIENNED ORANGE ZEST, FOR GARNISH

In a heavy-bottomed saucepan, combine 3/4 cup of the heavy cream, the tea, cardamom, sugar, and salt. Over medium-low heat, whisk the ingredients until blended. Stirring often, heat until the mixture just begins to boil. Remove from the heat, and allow the cream to cool until it reaches room temperature, about 15 minutes.

In a small bowl, combine the remaining 1/4 cup heavy cream and the gelatin. Let stand until the gelatin softens and absorbs the liquid, about 10 minutes. In a small saucepan, heat the gelatin mixture over medium-low heat (or leave it in the bowl and heat it in the microwave) until the gelatin dissolves and the mixture is hot but not boiling. Set aside.

In a large bowl, whisk the sour cream until smooth. Pour the tea mixture and the gelatin mixture through a sieve into the sour cream and stir until smooth and well blended. Pour the mixture into a pitcher and let it cool to room temperature. Stir to blend, and divide the mixture among six 4-ounce demitasse cups or small dessert cups. Chill for several hours until set, or as long as overnight.

To serve, drizzle 1 or 2 teaspoons of Orange Honey Sauce on top of each dessert. Garnish with 2 or 3 slivers of orange zest.

savories

. . .

a tea sandwich medley

From the Mad Hatter's tabletop to Buckingham Palace, delicate sandwiches gracefully eaten with the fingers have long been a delightful part of afternoon tea. Originally designed to tide a person over until the dinner hour, the tea sandwiches were eaten first, before the warm scones and sweet pastries. While traditional tea sandwiches use two slices of bread, we also include open-faced sandwiches that appeal to a streamlined sense of spontaneity and fun. ❖ Here are guidelines and suggestions for simple fillings and spreads as well as four tasty and attractive open-faced tea sandwiches.

simple fillings and spreads

- ❖ Avocado with sprouts and chopped toasted hazelnuts with cream cheese on white bread
- ❖ Chopped hard-boiled egg and watercress on whole wheat bread
- ❖ Cucumber and radish slices with cream cheese on white bread
- ❖ Cucumber slices on a spread of cream cheese and watercress, sprinkled with crumbled feta on white bread
- ❖ Pear slices with cream cheese, sprinkled with crumbled Roquefort on oatmeal bread
- ❖ Smoked salmon on cream cheese with caviar on brown bread
- ❖ Toasted walnuts with cream cheese on raisin bread
- ❖ Tomato and basil with cream cheese on whole wheat bread

for little sweethearts

- ❖ Apple slices on chocolate hazelnut spread (Nutella) on raisin bread
- ❖ Apple slices on cheese slice, sprinkled with cinnamon on toasted English muffin
- ❖ Cream cheese, brown sugar, and chopped apple on white bread

guidelines

❖ Use thin-sliced bread. Traditional sandwiches are made with thin-sliced white or whole wheat bread and are $5/8$ inch thick. (If necessary, you can order special, thin-sliced tea sandwich bread from a bakery.) On average, half of a 1-pound loaf will yield 10 to 12 regular sandwiches, which can be cut into 40 to 48 squares or 30 to 36 rectangular sandwiches. (If open-faced, the yield is doubled.)

❖ For uniform shapes, use a serrated knife to cut up to 6 slices of bread at once. First remove the crusts, and then cut into rectangles, squares, or triangles. For novelty shapes, use a biscuit cutter or cookie cutter to cut 2 slices at once.

❖ Always spread each piece of bread with room-temperature butter, cream cheese, or a combination of the two. This seals the filling and prevents the sandwich from becoming soggy. To cover 10 to 12 open-faced sandwiches adequately , you will need $1/3$ cup of spread.

❖ Keep fillings simple. For 10 to 12 open-faced sandwiches, you will need $1/2$ cup of soft, spreadable filling 1 or more cups for coarser fillings, and $3/4$ pound of sliced meats.

❖ To keep the bread from drying out, cover the slices with plastic wrap or a damp cloth while you make the sandwiches.

(continued)

1 SLICE THIN, CRUSTLESS PUMPERNICKEL
BREAD, APPROXIMATELY 2^1/$_2$ BY 2^1/$_2$ INCHES

CREAM CHEESE SPREAD

THINLY SLICED LOX, CUT TO FIT THE BREAD

SLIVERS OF RED ONION

MINCED FRESH DILL, FOR GARNISH

1 SLICE THIN, CRUSTLESS RAISIN BREAD,
APPROXIMATELY 2^1/$_2$ BY 2^1/$_2$ INCHES

BUTTER OR CREAM CHEESE AT ROOM
TEMPERATURE

PEANUT SPREAD

THIN SLICE OF COOKED CHICKEN BREAST,
CUT TO SIZE

THIN SLICE OF MELON BALL, CUT TO SIZE

MINCED CILANTRO LEAVES, FOR GARNISH

1 SLICE THIN, CRUSTLESS WHITE BREAD,
CUT INTO THE DESIRED SHAPE,
APPROXIMATELY 2^1/$_2$ BY 2^1/$_2$ INCHES

BUTTER OR CREAM CHEESE AT ROOM
TEMPERATURE

OLIVE TAPENADE SPREAD

2 MATCHSTICK SLICES PEELED JICAMA

2 SLIVERS ROASTED RED PEPPER

lox and cream cheese tea sandwich

Lightly spread the bread with a thin layer of the cream cheese spread. Top with a slice of lox and slivers of red onion. Garnish with minced dill.

cream cheese spread: In a small bowl, blend ^{1}/$_4$ cup cream cheese, ^{1}/$_2$ teaspoon white pepper, and 1^1/$_2$ teaspoons fresh lemon juice together. Chill any unused spread for up to 2 weeks. Makes about ^{1}/$_4$ cup, enough for 10 to 12 sandwiches.

chicken satay tea sandwich

Lightly spread the bread with butter or cream cheese. Next, lightly spread with the peanut spread. Top with chicken and a wedge of melon. Sprinkle with cilantro.

peanut spread: In a small bowl, blend ^{1}/$_4$ cup creamy-style peanut butter, 2 table-spoons hoisin sauce, 1 tablespoon soy sauce, 1 tablespoon ketchup, and 1 table-spoon hot water together. Add Tabasco sauce or chili sauce to taste. Chill any unused spread for up to 2 weeks. (Leftover spread makes a tasty raw vegetable dip.) Makes about ^{1}/$_2$ cup, enough for 12 to 14 sandwiches.

olive tapenade tea sandwich

Lightly spread the bread with butter or cream cheese. Next, lightly spread with the tapenade, leaving a clean, exposed rim of white bread. Garnish the top with 4 alternating slivers of jicama and red pepper.

olive tapenade spread: In a food chopper or processor, combine 3 ounces pitted black olives, ^{1}/$_2$ teaspoon anchovy paste, 1 tablespoon capers, 2 teaspoons olive oil, and 1 small clove garlic. Process to a coarse paste. Chill any unused spread for up to 2 weeks. Makes about ^{1}/$_3$ cup, enough for 10 to 12 sandwiches.

shrimp curry tea sandwich

1 SLICE THIN, CRUSTLESS WHITE BREAD,
   APPROXIMATELY 2$\frac{1}{2}$ BY 2$\frac{1}{2}$ INCHES

BUTTER OR CREAM CHEESE AT ROOM
TEMPERATURE

CURRY MAYONNAISE SPREAD

SLICE OF PEELED CUCUMBER

1 SMALL TO MEDIUM COOKED SHRIMP,
   WHOLE OR SLICED IN HALF LENGTHWISE

CHUTNEY

HERB LEAF OR LEAF TIP, FOR GARNISH

Lightly spread the bread with butter or cream cheese. Next, lightly spread it with curry mayonnaise. Top with the cucumber slice and shrimp. Spoon a dollop of chutney into the inside curve of the shrimp. Garnish with herb leaf.

curry mayonnaise spread: In a small bowl, blend $\frac{1}{4}$ cup mayonnaise, $\frac{1}{2}$ teaspoon curry powder, and $\frac{1}{2}$ teaspoon fresh lemon juice together. Use immediately, or cover and chill until needed. Makes about $\frac{1}{4}$ cup, enough for 10 to 12 sandwiches.

smoked ham tea biscuit

1 SAVORY SCONE BISCUIT (PAGE 79)

MUSTARD MAYONNAISE SPREAD

2 THIN SLICES HICKORY-SMOKED HAM,
   CUT TO FIT THE BISCUIT

Cut each biscuit in half widthwise. Lightly cover the cut side of each half with a thin layer of mustard mayonnaise spread. Top one half with the ham. Top with the other biscuit half, spread side down.

mustard mayonnaise spread: In a small bowl, blend $\frac{1}{4}$ cup mayonnaise and 1 tablespoon Dijon-style mustard together. Chill any unused spread for up to 2 weeks. Makes about $\frac{1}{4}$ cup, enough for 10 to 12 sandwiches.

lapsang souchong
sea scallops with asian slaw

Serves 4

Larry Kirkland, one of the most inventive cooks I know, developed this delicious recipe for marinating sea scallops in an aromatic brew of Lapsang Souchong tea. The tea imparts its marvelous smoky flavor to the scallops. In this recipe, the scallops serve as a first course and are accompanied with a crisp Asian slaw.

scallops

3   CUPS WATER

1/2   CUP LOOSE LAPSANG SOUCHONG TEA
      LEAVES

1   POUND SEA SCALLOPS, SMALL, TOUGH
    MUSCLES REMOVED

dressing

2   TABLESPOONS WATER

1/4   CUP SUGAR

1/4   CUP FISH SAUCE

1   TABLESPOON FRESH LIME JUICE

1   CLOVE GARLIC, MINCED

asian slaw

2   CUPS SHREDDED CABBAGE

1/2   CUP SHREDDED CARROTS

1/2   SMALL RED BELL PEPPER, CORED, SEEDED,
      AND THINLY SLICED

1/4   CUP THINLY SLICED RED ONION

1/4   CUP FRESH MINT LEAVES, TORN INTO SMALL
      PIECES AND LOOSELY PACKED

1/4   CUP FRESH BASIL LEAVES, TORN INTO SMALL
      PIECES AND LOOSELY PACKED

1/4   CUP FINELY CHOPPED UNSALTED PEANUTS,
      FOR GARNISH

4   MINT OR BASIL LEAVES, FOR GARNISH

4   LIME WEDGES, FOR GARNISH

to prepare the scallops: In a saucepan, bring the water to a boil and add the tea leaves. Cover and steep for 5 minutes. Strain the tea, discarding the leaves, and set aside to cool.

Place the scallops in a glass baking dish and cover with the cooled tea. Marinate for 30 to 60 minutes. With a slotted spoon, remove the scallops and pat dry on paper towels. Reserve the tea.

Pour the reserved tea into a 12-inch soup kettle, wok, or skillet. Place a steamer rack (or jerry-rig a cake rack) in the skillet, making sure the rack does not touch the liquid. Bring the tea to a full boil. Place the scallops on the rack, cover with a tight lid, and steam for 7 minutes. Remove the scallops and set aside.

to prepare the dressing: In a small jar with a lid, combine the water and sugar. Shake until the sugar dissolves. Add the fish sauce, lime juice, and garlic. Cover and shake. Makes about 2/3 cup.

to prepare the slaw: In a salad bowl, toss the cabbage, carrots, bell pepper, onion, mint, and basil together until blended. Add dressing to taste.

To serve, place 2/3 to 3/4 cup slaw on each of 4 small plates. Garnish with chopped nuts. Arrange 2 or 3 scallops on the plate and garnish with whole mint or basil leaves and a thin wedge of lime.

chinese tea eggs

Makes 6 to 10 eggs

Everything about these eggs will surprise you, especially how good they taste. Plus, they look spectacular (and kids will be fascinated by their raku-crackled glaze). Dusted with a combination of toasted sesame seeds and coarse salt, the eggs make an excellent hors d'oeuvre.

3   TO 4 CUPS COLD WATER

6   TO 10 EGGS

2   TABLESPOONS BLACK TEA LEAVES

2   TEASPOONS CHINESE FIVE-SPICE POWDER

1   TABLESPOON FLEUR DE SEL, KOSHER
    SALT, OR ANY LARGE-GRAIN SALT

In a pot large enough to hold the eggs without crowding, cover the eggs with the water. Over medium heat, bring the water to a gentle boil. Simmer the eggs for 12 minutes. With a strainer or slotted spoon, remove the eggs and place them in a cold-water bath until they can be easily handled. Reserve the cooking water. With the back of a spoon, lightly tap each shell all over until it is covered with a cobweb of cracks.

Bring the water used to cook the eggs back to a boil. Add the tea leaves, five-spice powder, and salt. With a slotted spoon, add the eggs. Cover, turn the heat to low, and simmer for 1 hour. Remove the pot from the heat. Keep the eggs in the covered pot to steep for 30 minutes. Remove the eggs from the water, and allow to cool.

To serve, shell the eggs. Eat whole, halved lengthwise, or quartered. Their flavor is best enjoyed within 24 hours.

jasmine tea eggs: For a fragrant, citrus-scented variation, simply follow the recipe for Chinese Tea Eggs, substituting Jasmine tea for the black tea and substituting the peel of an orange for the five-spice powder. (Use a vegetable peeler to peel the orange just as you would peel an apple. Try not to take any of the white pith.) Proceed as directed.

sensational tea-smoked chicken

Serves 4

Smoking with tea is a traditional Chinese approach to preparing chicken. The darkened skin and smoky flavor that result evokes Cajun-style cuisine. Even though the procedure may seem a bit daunting, it's really quite easy, and the flavor of the chicken is irresistible.

3   CLOVES GARLIC, CHOPPED

1   TABLESPOON GRATED PEELED FRESH
      GINGER ROOT

1   TABLESPOON HONEY

¾ CUP SOY SAUCE

½ CUP SHERRY

10 TO 20 CHICKEN WING DRUMETTES

1   CUP FIRMLY PACKED BROWN SUGAR

1   CUP LAPSANG SOUCHONG TEA LEAVES

SESAME SEEDS, FOR GARNISH

In a small bowl, mix the garlic, ginger root, honey, soy sauce, and sherry together. Pour the marinade into a 9-by-13-inch baking pan or a sealable quart-sized plastic freezer bag, and add the chicken. Coat the chicken well with the marinade. Refrigerate for at least 2 hours, tossing or rotating the chicken several times.

To smoke the chicken, choose a heavy cast-iron Dutch oven, roasting pan, or skillet with a tight-fitting lid. (Because of possible staining, use an old Dutch oven or pan.) Line the entire pan with heavy-duty aluminum foil. Sprinkle the brown sugar and tea in the foil-lined bottom. Place a wire cake rack (see Note) in the pan, over the sugar and tea mixture. Arrange the wings on the rack. If necessary, stack them in 2 layers. Cover the pan with a lid. Press the foil overhang against the lid for a snug fit. Turn on your kitchen exhaust fan to high.

Place the pan over medium-high to high heat for 30 minutes. (The temperature is high enough when you see little wisps of smoke escaping from the foil.) Do not remove the lid to check. After 30 minutes, turn off the heat and keep the chicken covered for an additional 20 minutes.

Remove and arrange on a serving plate. Garnish with sesame seeds. Serve warm or at room temperature.

note: It may be necessary to cut the wire rack to fit or to make your own using galvanized hardware cloth. ✤ As with any recipe that is cooked over high heat, use extreme caution. This dish produces smoke, it is imperative that you use your exhaust fan and that the pan or skillet has a tight-fitting lid. (As a good safety measure have a kitchen fire extinguisher.)

personal spa: herbal and tea blends

. . .

Many of the teas, herbs, and spices you savor as beverages can transform your daily beauty routine into a refreshing interlude. Even nicer, you can easily make these lovely and relaxing bath sachets, sweet-smelling soaps, eye pillows, and potpourris yourself. Bathtime becomes a relaxing spa treatment when you luxuriate in these aromatic tea and herbal blends of dried leaves and flowers.

Here are five simple blends made almost entirely from tea, kitchen herbs, and pantry spices, which you will use in the personal spa and potpourri recipes that follow. Each blend also has a suggested complementary essential oil that will intensify the fragrance in several of the recipes. As with any tea or herbal blends, after you have tried these, experiment and create your own.

green chai tea blend

Makes 1 cup tea blend

¼ CUP CHINESE GREEN TEA LEAVES

¼ CUP WHOLE GREEN CARDAMOM PODS

¼ CUP WHOLE CLOVES

3 OR 4 THREE-INCH CINNAMON STICKS, COARSELY CHOPPED WITH A HEAVY-DUTY KNIFE

(ESSENTIAL OIL COMPLEMENT: ORANGE)

In a quart-sized plastic bag, place the tea leaves, cardamom, cloves, and cinnamon sticks. Blow into the bag as if blowing up a balloon. Once it's inflated, hold the bag shut and shake until well combined. Store in a clean, opaque glass or ceramic jar with a screwtop lid or tight-fitting cork. Give the jar a good shake to help distribute the different ingredients before removing any tea. For peak fragrance, use within 6 months. (The essential oil can be used in the recipes that follow.)

four-flower herbal tea blend: Follow the recipe for Green Chai Tea Blend, using ¼ cup dried chamomile flowers, ¼ cup dried hop flowers, ¼ cup dried lavender flowers, and ¼ cup dried rose petals. (*Essential oil complement: lavender.*)

aromatic herbal tea blend: Follow the recipe for Green Chai Tea Blend, using ⅓ cup dried lavender flowers, ⅓ cup dried peppermint leaves, and ⅓ cup dried rose petals. (*Essential oil complement: rose.*)

soothing herbal tea blend: Follow the recipe for Green Chai Tea Blend, using ⅓ cup dried chamomile flowers, ⅓ cup dried hops, and ⅓ cup dried marjoram leaves. (*Essential oil complement: chamomile.*)

stimulating herbal tea blend: Follow the recipe for Green Chai, using ⅓ cup dried eucalyptus leaves, ⅓ cup dried lemon balm leaves, and ⅓ cup dried rosemary leaves. (*Essential oil complement: eucalyptus.*)

steeping beauty bath tea sachet

Makes 1 bath tea sachet

Nourish body and soul with a relaxing, hot bath scented with aromatic tea and herbal blends. If you make extra sachets, you can fill a small basket or tray and leave it in the bathroom to fill the room with their heavenly fragrance.

½ CUP GREEN CHAI TEA BLEND OF YOUR CHOICE (PAGE 109)

4 OR 5 DROPS COMPLEMENTARY ESSENTIAL OIL (OPTIONAL; SEE SPECIFIC BLEND)

materials needed:

10- TO 12-INCH SQUARE FINELY WOVEN, LIGHTWEIGHT HANDKERCHIEF, MUSLIN, OR CLOTH NAPKIN

1 TWO-INCH RUBBER BAND

2 YARDS SATIN OR GROSGRAIN RIBBON, ¼ INCH WIDE

Lay the fabric square on a clean, flat surface. Place the tea blend in the center of the handkerchief. Sprinkle the blend with essential oil, if desired. Pick up each of the four corners, bringing the points together. Holding the points in one hand, use your free hand to gather and hold the fabric in the center, just above the tea. Secure the fabric with the rubber band.

Wrap the ribbon once around the rubber band. Tie with a secure knot and make a bow. Bring the ends of the ribbon straight up from the bow. Holding the ends together, tie another knot and bow, about 18 inches above the first bow.

At bath time, hang the sachet over the tap so that the warm water will run through the bag, or swish it around in the hot water. The long ribbon loop allows the sachet to stay immersed in the water during the bath. The sachet is good for several baths.

soothing salts sachet: Enhance your sachet with the soothing properties of Epsom salts. Follow the recipe for Steeping Beauty Bath Tea Sachet, mixing ½ cup Epsom salts with the tea blend. Proceed as directed.

the pleasures of tea potpourri

Makes 1 cup potpourri

There is something delightful about walking into a room filled with the fragrant air of potpourri. To make your own, follow this simple recipe. You can be as creative as you like in selecting the blends and essential oils. The most important thing to remember is to use the best ingredients you can find.

1 CUP GREEN CHAI TEA BLEND OF YOUR CHOICE (PAGE 109)

1 TO 2 TEASPOONS POWDERED ORRISROOT (AVAILABLE AT DRUG STORES OR WHERE HERBAL SUPPLIES ARE SOLD)

8 TO 10 DROPS COMPLEMENTARY ESSENTIAL OIL (SEE SPECIFIC BLEND)

In a quart-sized plastic bag, place the tea blend and orrisroot. Blow into the bag as if blowing up a balloon. Once it's inflated, hold the bag shut and shake until the mixture is blended. Open the bag and add the essential oil. Inflate again and shake. Store in a clean, opaque glass or ceramic jar with a screwtop lid or tight-fitting cork for 4 to 6 weeks to cure. Give the jar a good shake to help distribute the different ingredients before removing the potpourri. After it has cured, the potpourri is ready to be placed into a decorative container. For peak fragrance, use enough potpourri to fill the container to the brim.

To refresh potpourri when the fragrance has faded, add a few drops of essential oil. How much is enough? Think of it as adding seasoning to a cooking recipe. Start with less and add more if needed. Also, gently stir the potpourri. This will break or crush petals and leaves and release more scent.

sweet citrus potpourri: Adding dried lemon or orange slices to potpourri gives it a lovely texture, added aroma, and visual appeal. I like to add dried lemon slices to the Soothing Herbal Tea Blend and dried orange slices to the Green Chai Tea Blend. To dry lemon or orange slices, preheat the oven to 175°F. Position a rack in the center of the oven. Line a baking sheet with parchment paper or aluminum foil. Cut off and discard the rind on both ends of the fruit, exposing the flesh. Carefully cut the fruit into eight to ten 1/8-inch slices. Place the slices on the baking sheet. Bake until dry but not brown, 2 to 3 hours. The rind will have the look of glassine. Remove from the oven and cool completely, turning the slices occasionally. To use, add the slices after the potpourri has cured.

eye love tea pillows

Makes 2 eye pillows

Pamper and refresh weary eyes with these soothing eye compresses that help reduce eye fatigue and puffiness. ✤ In a hurry? For a quick-as-a-wink refresher, instead of making your own compress, you can use herbal tea bags—the same ones you would use in a beverage. Simply follow the technique described below.

¼ CUP GREEN CHAI TEA BLEND OF YOUR
    CHOICE (PAGE 109)

materials needed:

SHEET OF TYPING PAPER, FOLDED IN HALF

2 MUSLIN TEA BAGS (SEE NOTE)

Using the folded paper as a funnel, divide the tea blend between the 2 muslin bags. Close each bag and secure with a tight knot and bow.

To release the tea's aroma and therapeutic properties, soak and saturate the bags in warm water for 2 minutes. Squeeze out the excess moisture. Place the moistened bags in a plastic storage container and chill for 10 to 20 minutes.

Make yourself comfortable and lay the chilled bags on your closed eyelids for 10 to 30 minutes.

note: 100 percent cotton gauze or muslin tea and sachet bags with drawstring ties are available at tea and coffee stores, cooking and craft stores, or from mail-order catalogs or Web sites (see "Resources," page 117).

teatime beauty soap

Makes 1 bar beauty soap

You can easily create your own exquisite beauty soap sans fancy packaging, chic logo, and high price tag. With a gentle abrasive quality that is kind to all skin types, Teatime Soap will leave your skin smooth, cleansed, and pleasantly fragrant.

1   FIVE-OUNCE BAR CASTILE OR VEGETABLE
    OIL SOAP

1/3 CUP BREWED TEA (ANY KIND) OR WATER

1/4 CUP GREEN CHAI TEA BLEND OF YOUR
    CHOICE (PAGE 109)

6   TO 8 DROPS COMPLEMENTARY
    ESSENTIAL OIL (SEE SPECIFIC BLEND)

materials needed:

HANDHELD GRATER

ENAMEL SAUCEPAN

EMPTY PINT MILK CARTON, CUT TO A HEIGHT
    OF 4 INCHES

PLASTIC WRAP

WAXED PAPER

CITRUS ZESTER

Using the large holes of a grater, grate the soap into the saucepan. Add the brewed tea and gently heat over medium-low until the soap has softened, stirring occasionally with a wooden spoon. Remove from the heat and cool until easy to touch, about 10 minutes. Knead with your hands to make a smooth paste. Sprinkle the tea blend and oil over the paste and continue to knead until blended. Let rest for 10 minutes.

Press the soap mixture evenly into the milk carton and cover the top of the soap with plastic wrap. Let stand for 2 hours. Remove the plastic wrap and tear away the carton mold. Using your hands, smooth the sides and edges of the soap. Cover with plastic wrap and let rest in a warm, dry spot for 24 hours. Discard the plastic wrap, rewrap the soap in waxed paper, and store in a warm, dry place for 1 month before using. For a decorative textured finish, pull a zester over each of the soap's 6 sides.

resources

There are many excellent sources of tea and accessories, guides to tea, retail businesses, and teahouses. I have listed a few that I have enjoyed and found helpful and informative. Use my suggestions as a jumping-off point for your own exploration.

BOOKS

Chow, Kit, and Ione Kramer. *All the Tea in China*. San Francisco: China Books and Periodicals, Inc., 1990.

Kowalchik, Claire, and William Hylton (editors). *Rodale's Illustrated Encylopedia of Herbs*. Emmaus, Pennsylvania: Rodale Books, 1987.

Mitscher, Lester, and Victoria Dolby. *The Green Tea Book*. New York: Avery Publishing Group, 1996.

Ody, Penelope. *Home Herbal*. London: Dorling Kindersley, 1995.

Podreka, Tomislav. *Serendipitea*. New York: William Morrow and Company, Inc., 1998.

The Republic of Tea. *The Book of Tea & Herbs*. Santa Rosa: The Cole Group, 1993.

Schapira, Joel, David Schapira, and Karl Schapira. *The Book of Coffee and Tea, second edition*. New York: St. Martin's Press, 1982.

TEAS, TEA ACCESSORIES, AND WEB SITES

As a general rule, the best place to purchase your tea is from a local tea merchant. That way, you're getting one-on-one professional attention, and can judge the freshness of the tea firsthand. When that is not possible, here are some other resources.

On the World Wide Web, there are undoubtedly thousands of sites that deal with tea. I've listed a few, but take stime to discover your own using Yahoo!, Google, Alltheweb, or AskJeeves.

harney & sons
www.harney.com
11 East Main Street
Village Green, P.O. Box 638
Salisbury, CT 06068
T. 888. 427. 6398
Fine teas and accesories from around the world, including Yixing ware, Brown Betty teapots, and cozies.

in pursuit of tea
www.inpursuitoftea.com
T. 866.878.382, toll free
Sebastian Beckwith explores remote regions of the world to supply his customers with fine true teas. The site is easy to navigate and informative. The online store has over 30 teas available by the quarter pound.

peet's coffee & tea
www.peets.com
1400 Park Avenue
Emeryville, CA 94608
T. 510. 594. 2100 or
    800. 999. 2132
This specialty coffee company has an exceptional line of teas that can be ordered by mail, by fax, or online.

the republic of tea
www.sipbysip.com
8 Digital Drive, Suite 100
Novato, CA 94949
T. 800. 298. 4832
The Web site takes a little practice to navigate. Besides an interesting array of teas, accessories available online include the Bodum Plunger-Pot Teapot.

serendipitea
www.serendipitea.com
P.O. Box 81
Ridgefield, CT 06877
T. 888. TEA LIFE or
    203. 894. 9650
An exquisite but limited selction of prime teas. Clever accessories.

Stash

www.stashtea.com
P.O. Box 910
Portland, OR 97207
T. 503. 684. 4482 or
    800. 547. 1514
One of the best tea-information
Web sites around, easy to navigate, and a treat to visit anytime.

teas of green

www.teasofgreen.com
This Web site was created by
Larry and Sachiko Ormsby of
Berkeley, California. For anyone
wanting to explore the world of
green tea, begin here. They have
excellent teas, good information,
and some lovely tea sets.

ten ren tea and ginseng co.

www.tenren.com
75 Mott Street
New York, NY 10013
T. 212. 349. 2286 or
    800. 292. 2049
Founded in Taiwan in 1953,
this company has expanded
to more than 100 retail stores
worldwide. Their online products
include a large array of tea
and ginseng products, including
sweets. There's green tea pie,
cookies, and caramels as well
as ginseng candy.

TEAHOUSES

angelina

226 Rue de Rivoli
Paris, France
www.angelina.fr
01. 4260. 8200

babington's tea rooms

Piazza di Spagna 23
Rome, Italy
06. 678. 6027

brown's hotel

33 Albemarle Street
Mayfair, London
www.brownshotel.com
020. 7518. 4108

claridge's

Brook Street
Mayfair, London
www.savoy-group.co.uk
020. 7629. 8860

empress hotel

721 Government Street
Victoria, B.C. V8W 1W5
www.theempresshotel.com
250. 384. 8111

imperial tea court

1411 Powell Street
San Francisco, CA 94133
(also Seattle, WA; other locations) www.imperialtea.com
415. 788. 6080 or
800. 567. 5898

ladurée

16 Rue Royale
Paris, France
42. 60. 21. 79

little teahouse

British Columbia (various locations) catteacorner.com/canada;
serves bubble iced tea, a fruit
and tea beverage made with
tapico pearls

tao of tea

3430 SE Belmont
Portland, OR 97214
www.taooftea.com
503. 736. 0119

tea & sympathy

108-110 Greenwich Avenue
New York, NY 10011
212. 807. 8329

tea box cafe at takashimaya

693 Fifth Avenue
New York, NY 10022
212. 350. 0100 or
800. 753. 2038

teaism, a teahouse

2009 R Street NW
Washington, DC. 20009 (other
locations) www.teaism.com
212. 667. 3827 or
888. 883. 2476

tealuxe

Zero Brattle Street
Harvard Square
Cambridge, MA 02138
(other locations, New York City)
www.tealuxe.com
617. 441. 0077

tearoom t

1568 W. Broadway
Vancouver, B.C. V6J 1W6
604. 878. 3000

general index

recipe index

table of equivalents

The exact equivalents in the following tables have been rounded for convenience.

LIQUID/DRY MEASURES

U.S.		metric	
1/4	teaspoon	1.25	milliliters
1/2	teaspoon	2.5	milliliters
1	teaspoon	5	milliliters
1	tablespoon (3 teaspoons)	15	milliliters
1	fluid ounce (2 tablespoons)	30	milliliters
1/4	cup	60	milliliters
1/3	cup	80	milliliters
1/2	cup	120	milliliters
1	cup	240	milliliters
1	pint (2 cups)	480	milliliters
1	quart (4 cups, 32 ounces)	960	milliliters
1	gallon (4 quarts)	3.84	liters
1	ounce (by weight)	28	grams
1	pound	454	grams
2.2	pounds	1	kilogram

OVEN TEMPERATURE

Fahrenheit	Celsius	Gas
250	120	1/2
275	140	1
300	150	2
325	160	3
350	180	4
375	190	5
400	200	6
425	220	7
450	230	8
475	240	9
500	260	10

LENGTH

U.S.		metric	
1/8	inch	3	millimeters
1/4	inch	6	millimeters
1/2	inch	12	millimeters
1	inch	2.5	centimeters